MW01488914

A Better Tomorrow

Millennial Mind Publishing
An imprint of American Book Publishing
5442 So. 900 East, #146
Salt Lake City, UT 84117-7204
www.american-book.com
Printed in the United States of America on acid-free paper.

A Better Tomorrow
Designed by Jana Rade, design@american-book.com

Publisher's Note: American Book Publishing relies on the author's integrity of research and attribution; each statement has not been investigated to determine if it has been accurately made. The author and publisher specifically disclaim any responsibility for any liability, loss, or risk, personal or otherwise, which is incurred as a consequence, directly or indirectly, of the use and application of any of the contents of this book. In such situations where medical, legal, or other professional services may apply, please seek the advice of such professionals directly.

ISBN-13: 978-1-58982-614-4
ISBN-10: 1-58982-614-0

Library of Congress Cataloging-in-Publication Data available by request.
E-mail info@american-book.com.

Special Sales: These books are available at special discounts for bulk purchases. Special editions, including personalized covers, excerpts of existing books, and corporate imprints, can be created in large quantities for special needs. For more information e-mail info@american-book.com.

A Better Tomorrow

Thomas Finn

Table of Contents

Introduction

This work does not pretend to be an expert analysis of the working of the subconscious mind and how it can transform our lives. Rather, it is a layman's account of his interest in these matters and the results of his research and efforts to improve his state in life. If the knowledge that I have gained and tested can benefit others, then this book will have fulfilled its purpose. It has been a long but eventful journey leading me to this point in time where I can look at the material written about self improvement and say with conviction that a certain method works extremely well.

Hopefully, I can save some people time by cutting to the chase and relating to them what I found best and most effective in my own quest for a better life. In the following pages, I go through my experiences and the methods I used to bring about changes in my own life. Some self-help books contain very important and helpful material, but one must wade through a forest of technical and theoretical facts and heavy detail before finally isolating the relevant ones. In my readings and research over the years, I have come across theories and assertions that I first thought were either off the mark or over exaggerated. As I continued to read, I realized that some theories were indeed over the top but others, which at first did not make a great deal of sense, were very valuable and practical. It was a long and thoughtful road, but eventually it became an education achieved the hard way. Because of this, my perception of the subconscious mind and its limitless potential radically changed my convictions and my life. It really amazed me that something so explosive and life changing is at our fingertips for our use and benefit. It is so easily mastered, and yet the vast majority of us do not submit to its awesome power.

Some people, who desperately need change in their lives or fortunes, feel there is no way out of their predicament. They say they feel trapped and cannot find a resolution to their problem and they sink lower into depression and misery. However, if they want to change, they must have a lot of perseverance and a certain degree of blind faith because life is never consistent. Life is full of change and when they are using the methods I have found successful they will attract the very changes that will solve their problems, given time and patience. Your feelings of hopelessness about your present predicament should not deter you. Circumstances change, and if you are influencing your subconscious in the correct way you will find these circumstances shifting just the right amount to grant you your dearest wishes. I firmly believe that most people allow their subconscious to be their master rather than their servant. This mindset leads to all kinds of stress and problems in their lives.

The following pages will explain how you can mold the subconscious mind to be like the genie in the bottle, making your wishes come true. It is similar to ticking off on a menu what characteristics and qualities you wish for most and knowing with certainty that these can and will be yours. This is not a far-fetched analogy; it may be simplifying things somewhat, but essentially it is accurate and I have proven it to be true for myself. I have been affirming now for a number of years at different levels of intensity and, though it may sound cliché, I believe my life has been transformed into an exciting adventure as I eagerly look forward to the next new chapter. The one change that I have derived the most satisfaction from is the fact that I actually like and respect myself now. In the past I lacked a positive self-image and my self-esteem was pretty low. If you can get your sleeping giant, better known as your subconscious, to work for you, then most things are possible. Only your own mind and beliefs will limit you. Aim high and have the vision to secure a better life for yourself. You will not regret it.

Before you even begin to start on your life-changing journey, one important condition must be made crystal clear; do not even think of taking the first steps on the road of improvement and change unless you are absolutely dedicated to the cause. You will not be doing yourself justice if you are not prepared to persevere to the very end. You will have to steel yourself for a long journey with many a twist and turn on the way and many doubts arising from time to time. However, if you are aware of the life changing benefits that can come your way and are totally committed, then you are bound to succeed. Good luck!

Chapter 1
The Awakening

Bring out the magic of your subconscious mind. Miracles will happen to you if only you will allow it. The master of success is your creative mind. Think and grow rich. Grow rich while you sleep; the secret of success.

All these emotive titles and sentences have been read by most of us at different times in our lives. They instantly appeal to our basic instincts and make us want to find out more about these wonderful claims. We cannot wait to try out these wonderful formulae for success. We either do the course or buy the book and eagerly anticipate an overnight success. We feel that being successful is almost too easy and scarcely believe our luck in having come across such secrets. We work away, full of enthusiasm and wait for the expected improvement and transformation. As nothing appears to be happening we are undaunted and work even harder for the magic to begin. Again nothing appears to be happening and we begin to wonder if we are doing this the right way. It has been emphasized time and time again that we must have an unshakable faith and belief in this system for it to work. Doubt begins to creep in. Do we really have a deep cast iron belief or do we just think that we do? We ignore these niggling doubts and we try to persevere with our positive thinking. It is no use. We do not seem to be any farther along the road to success than we were at the start. What a waste of time, not to mention money, to have read this book and done this course. We feel disheartened and disillusioned by the whole process and resent the people who are profiting out of such claims. What mugs we are! Does this sound familiar to you? Have you been there, done that? Everybody has, at some time in his or her life, undertaken some improvement course or gotten some tuition in bettering themselves. Only the very lazy or complacent person does not bother to better their station in life. Surely all the books and courses written about the magic of the mind cannot have been a cheap trick to make money. All these success stories could not have been made up, could they?

To answer, I will give you a brief résumé of my own experiences. I was always interested in self-improvement courses and self-help books, feeling I had a lot of improving to do to get up to par. I would start a course or read a book and be very enthusiastic at first, but eventually, give up for some reason or other. Usually this happened because I believed I was doing it wrong. A few years later I would repeat the same process with the same disappointing results. This was the pattern for much of my life. Every now and again I returned to the subject and wondered if I could use it to my advantage. Each time the method appeared under a different guise but the same principle remained.

Breakthrough

Positive-thinking, auto-suggestion, the law of attraction, self-suggestion, creative visualization, affirmations, manifesting, etc., all basically use the same principle for communicating with the subconscious on a deep level in order to transform oneself. The more I learned about the subconscious mind the more I realized that I was on the right track. Whatever I want to manifest in my life I must think about and believe in most strongly and imagine most vividly. It is often called the law of attraction. When we are negative about something we often attract that negativity. Conversely, if we project positively and expect and visualize happiness and satisfaction, we tend to attract that situation.

But why then, was I unsuccessful with my experimental methods? I had arrived at a stage in my life when I decided that I owed it to myself to make one last concerted effort to effect a profound change in my life. If this did not work, then there was something seriously wrong, either with me or else the system. I was determined to finally get an answer one way or the other. I went through many of the old books I had read over the years on influencing the subconscious mind. From them I learned that change in one's personality by conscious efforts is temporary, insignificant, and also bloody hard work. I already knew this from hard experience. I was now convinced that profound and permanent change is effected when the subconscious is coaxed and influenced in a subtle and deep manner.

This concept sounded simple yet difficult at the same time. I realized that, for real change to take place, the subconscious mind would have to receive powerful, irresistible commands that could not be ignored. These changes would manifest themselves in very subtle ways, gaining momentum like a rolling snowball. One would have no conscious control over these changes. I realized that a person's personality and behavior was largely the result of influences outside of their control. In some cases it may be in harmony with their aims in life. In other cases, however, it may be discordant and completely unharmonious, causing frustration, stress, unhappiness and disappointment. These influences are inhibitions holding one back from the full realization of their potential and are deeply hidden in the subconscious.

If you are happily reading a newspaper and you come across a disturbing headline, you may be gripped with shock and revulsion and quickly put it away. Thus, a force that, up to that point was unseen suddenly manifests itself and changes your behavior completely. This came from the subconscious and illustrates how we have little conscious control over the deeply held convictions of this part of our mind. You may feel that there are some past experiences causing inhibitions that act against your conscious aims and desires. If so, the good news is that not only can you control them, but you can also totally remove them. You can do this and substitute in their place powerful, positive forces that will strengthen your personality and guide you along the path you wish to travel. When an aim or definite goal is firmly planted in the subconscious, it begins to work ceaselessly to bring about that desired result until it is either achieved or a new goal replaces it. Remember, this happens completely independently of the conscious mind. The only time you become conscious of something happening is upon becoming aware of new exciting changes in your life.

When I was finally convinced of these explosive revelations, I knew I owed it to myself to seriously begin to transform my personality and state in life. I realized that I had been doing things correctly earlier on but lacked conviction. The next step was the actual mechanics of communicating directly to the subconscious. There are countless ways of influencing the subconscious mind for change and no doubt all these work for different people. Basically, it is horses for courses. It is important that one uses the particular method best suited to them. The one common unifier for all methods is that the subconscious mind has to be conditioned properly, and then targeted with emotive and stimulating commands or assertions. I have come across complicated spiritual methods that, if followed assiduously, would probably have produced results. Others, it appeared, would require impractical conditions. Some practices, for instance, entail long periods each day of relaxing in specific circumstances, which are difficult to create. A practitioner would need great flexibility, as well as, a lot of time and willpower. The danger with such a method is that, if results were not forthcoming many would become discouraged, which would be fatal.

Summary

1)   Most of us from time to time have read self-improvement books. We have put the theories into practice but generally have had disappointing results.

2)   We owe it to ourselves to find out why we aren't getting positive results.

3)   The law of attraction is a way of manifesting into our lives what we truly desire.

4)   Permanent change is affected when our subconscious mind is influenced in a deep, subtle manner.

5)   One's personality and behavior is largely the result of influences outside their control.

6) When one's conscious mind is not in harmony with the subconscious, frustration, stress and unhappiness result.

7) When an aim or goal is firmly planted in the subconscious, it continues working to bring about the desired result until it is achieved or a new goal replaces it.

8) Change happens completely independent of the conscious mind.

9) The subconscious mind has to be properly conditioned before being targeted with powerful commands or affirmations.

10) The chosen method of communicating with the subconscious mind must be one that best suits an individual's circumstances.

Inspirational Words

The following are some inspirational quotes I came across in my research and read over every now and again for inspiration and motivation. These I have proven truthful and helpful for myself, and thus, perhaps others.

"Whatever the mind can conceive and believe it can achieve."
--W. Clement Wattles

"A man is what he thinks about all day long."
--Ralph Waldo Emerson

"Change your thoughts and you change your world."
--Norman Vincent Peale

"For as he thinketh in his heart, so is he."
--Proverbs (23:7)

"We are what we repeatedly do. Excellence then is not an act but a habit."
--Aristotle

Chapter 2
My Way

After a few false starts I found the most effective way of influencing the subconscious mind was through emotional affirmations. This simple but sustained practice gently and persuasively coaxes the deepest thinking part of the mind similar to self-hypnosis. Emile Coué, the French psychologist and author of the book "Self-Mastery Through Conscious Autosuggestion" recommended that his pupils say, "Every day in every way I am getting better and better." Coué, who graduated in pharmacy, noticed that in certain cases he could improve the efficacy of a medicine simply by praising its effectiveness to the patient. He realized that those patients to whom he praised the medicine had a marked improvement over those patients to whom he said nothing. Apparently, he got some stunning results with this simple method. I began my rehabilitation by deciding what changes I most needed in my life and what I had often dreamt of but never believed possible. It was a bit like the magic genie in the bottle asking you for your wishes. I wrote out and tore up many different lists before I finally decided on my wish list. Even then, every now and again, I found myself altering the phrasing or wording on my list until I felt comfortable with it. You will know when an affirmation is right for you. You may be undecided for some time, but when the ideal sentence or phrase presents itself it will resonate with you, leaving you in no doubt that it is the correct one for you. Personally, I listed six changes or goals that I desired or wished for most.

During my research I paid special attention to the law of attraction and found the theory fascinating. You unconsciously attract most negative happenings in your life. Take health for instance. If you are always worrying about catching colds or some disease or other, then subconsciously you are unwittingly attracting the very thing you fear most. The moral here is to always focus on what you want to attain, not what you want to get away from. Personally, I found out that it was true. I always had been a bit of a pessimist and often what I was dreading did, in fact, happen to me. Now I know why.

The law of attraction, according to experts, is a law of nature and from my experience it is hard to disagree. All of us are constantly attracting by default, though unaware of it. We have an attitude to everything that goes on in our world and unconsciously have energized thoughts about everything that concerns us. Our thoughts and feelings are on autopilot, but that does not stop the attraction. You might say that it is impossible to monitor our thousands of thoughts every day and thus influence our attractions. This is, of course, very true. Do not despair, however; there is a very simple remedy: our feelings. Our feelings always let us know what we are thinking and can warn us if we are on the right track or not. Our emotions and feelings tell us very quickly if there is a green light and we can continue with our present thought pattern or, if the red light is flashing, we should stop immediately. It may take a little time and conscious effort at first to do a quick check every now and then. However, eventually, it will become automatic and we can quickly redirect our thoughts. If we feel bad and continue carrying on that way, we are in effect saying, *Fine, bring me more circumstances that will make me feel bad.*

On the other side of the coin, if we have good feelings and emotions like gratitude, love, joy, and happiness, we will attract more good feelings that make us happy. Factually, it is impossible to feel good if we have negative feelings. If we are feeling good it is due to good thoughts. The opposite is, of course, also true. Strive to sustain good or positive thoughts at all times and you will gain immense benefits from them. This is where the phrase "the power of positive thinking" comes from. I made a vow to concentrate on positive affirmations from then on, excluding anything negative. What you think about predominantly, you attract. Your thoughts, in fact, become your reality. This may sound something of a cliché but I have proven it to be true. I have found out the hard way that the best and most effective method of transmitting your thoughts to your subconscious is through repetition. One drop of rain will not affect a slab of limestone. However, this action repeated over a number of years will alter the shape of the slab considerably. A thought planted in the subconscious is similar to a seed planted in the fertile earth: nothing happens for a long time. However, beneath the surface the seed is transforming itself into a new plant and establishing a root system. With time and regular watering, a beautiful new plant emerges and quickly grows. Though a little biblical, it is patently true. A thought that is constantly repeated with feeling over a length of time will bear fruit and have a profound effect on our subconscious. The beneficial results often happen when least expected. That is why it is described as magical. I worked hard on doing my affirmations as often as I could during the day. Gradually, I found that some affirmations easily rolled off the tongue while I wasn't entirely comfortable with others. I continued to experiment until I found the words and sentences that most impacted and best expressed my desire.

Relaxation and Affirmations

Positive affirmations always influence and stimulate the deeper mind when repeated constantly during the day. Moreover, the subconscious mind is most sensitive to outside influences when the conscious one is least active. The conscious mind is often referred to as the gatekeeper of the subconscious, as it monitors everything that is passed through it. Thus, when the conscious mind is not on active duty, access to the subconscious is much easier. Relaxation is the key to unlocking the door to the deeper mind. Effective relaxation is easy to learn, and with a little practice, becomes second nature. Generally, people will affirm many times each day as they lead a busy life. Periods of relaxation are not always practical, but whenever possible they should compose themselves prior to affirmations. It is a scientific fact that when body and mind are deeply relaxed the brain wave pattern becomes different, slowing down substantially. This deep level is called the alpha level as opposed to the beta level, which is the waking consciousness. The alpha level is a very healthy state of consciousness as it relaxes the mind and body, which creates the perfect climate for profound change to take place using affirmations and visualization. From experience I have found the following steps in the relaxation process work very well:

-Make yourself as comfortable as possible either lying on a bed or reclining in a chair while keeping the back straight.

-Breathe slowly and deeply while becoming aware of the sound of your breathing. Continue until you can breathe easily and rhythmically.

-While breathing easily, gradually become aware of your muscles, allowing them to let go and relax. Start with the feet and work your way up through the body to the top of your head. After the feet, move to the legs and calf muscles, thighs, lower back, upper back, belly, chest, shoulders, arms, hands, fingers and neck. Allow your face muscles, jaw and forehead to loosen and go limp.

-Try to think of your body as a hot air balloon with the air being expelled or imagine that you are a limp rag doll. Some people like to compare themselves to a great block of concrete sinking down deeply onto the chair or bed.

-It may help to recall a tranquil scene from your memory such as a mountain view or maybe a boat out on a calm sea.

-When totally relaxed let your mind be occupied by a mental picture of yourself as you would like to be and acting as you would like to be. As you observe yourself in this situation, calmly and slowly repeat the affirmations you have chosen to reinforce the projected picture. For example repeat, *I am completely calm and deeply relaxed at all times.*

Do not worry about doubts that may creep into your mind because visualization and affirmations always work independently of the conscious mind. Just believe that it will happen and it will.

Some people think they have tried and failed with affirmations and visualization in influencing their deeper mind. If you are one of these, I assure you the chances are that you never got through to your subconscious. Many a man decides to change the way he'll live his life—but all he changes is his conscious mind. If you really want change in your life you must persevere, persevere, persevere and think of the hidden seed in the ground. You owe it to yourself.

Summary

1)   Personally, I find the best way of influencing the subconscious is through sustained emotional affirmations.

2)   Write down a wish list of the changes you would most like in your life. Rewrite the list until you are comfortable with the wording.

3)   Unconsciously, whether we like it or not, we attract to ourselves whatever circumstances or misfortunes we are burdened with.

4)   Our constant thoughts are what influence us in the long run.

5)   It is virtually impossible to monitor all our thoughts, but our feelings are the key to concentrating on the positive ones.

6)   Constant positive thoughts will bring immense and immeasurable benefits.

7)   I believe the only guaranteed way of transmitting your thoughts to the subconscious is by affirmation done repeatedly. There is no substitute for repetition.

8)   A thought constantly repeated with feeling over a length of time will have a profound effect on the subconscious.

9)   Access to the subconscious is most successful when body and mind are relaxed. Relaxation is the key to unlocking the door to the inner mind.

10) Have a routine in doing relaxation exercises each day. It may be strange and awkward at first, but it will become easier with practice.

Inspirational Words

"We ourselves feel that what we are doing is just a drop in the ocean. But the ocean would be less because of that missing drop."
--Mother Theresa

"Life is the sum of what you focus on."
--Winifred Gallagher

"The world will be balanced when we are balanced."
--Tarthang Tulku

"Our deeds determine us, as much as we determine our deeds."
--George Eliot

"Take care of the minutes and the hours will take care of themselves."
--Lord Chesterfield

Chapter 3
My Affirmations

Ideally, affirmations should be used during the day when most convenient. Everyone is different in this respect; it is very individually driven. To be most effective, they should be repeated in an emotional or animated way whether silently or aloud. Some people like to affirm aloud and aggressively in front of a mirror but they should be cautious to avoid embarrassment or a lot of explaining. Some like to walk around a large room while audibly affirming while others go for solitary walks as the isolation helps them to concentrate. You will eventually find what suits you best. Personally, I think the best and most effective, but not the most practical, way of affirming is to go into a warehouse and lock the door. There you can proceed to operate in peace and privacy. You can then bring as much feeling and emotions to your affirmations as you want without feeling inhibited in forcibly verbalizing these emotions. I believe the more animated, enthusiastic, emotional and fervent your affirmations are, the more impact they will have on your creative mind.

<u>Staying Power</u>

When I began using affirmations seriously, I determined to persevere until I procured positive results. I was as determined and resolute about the task at hand as anything I had done in my life. I knew that the stakes were high and the prize was big, so it was literally now or never. For quite a while I was religiously doing the affirmations but nothing appeared to be happening. Again the old doubts started to creep in and haunt me; I stubbornly kept persevering. I recalled reading an account of a mining company that spent a lot of time and money excavating for some precious mineral. Having had no success they conceded defeat and terminated work. A new replacement company almost immediately struck it rich only meters away from where the first company ceased operations. Fortified and inspired by the moral of this story, I continued with my efforts even though things did not look promising.

However, slowly, almost imperceptibly, something began to change. At first I thought it was just a coincidence or at best a temporary improvement, but no, the changes grew more noticeable and decidedly permanent. I felt empowered. Every time I took a step forward, that was it, there was no going back, no relapses. What ground I gained I kept. In other aspects of life improvement change is very often temporary, eventually returning to the status quo, but this never applies to a shift in the subconscious. I finally received what I always wanted: belief in myself, and, more importantly, belief in the validity of the system. The whole process became dreamlike to me. It almost seemed a little unreal. I found it hard to believe that I had finally cracked it. I felt stronger and finally in control of my life and destiny. Even though the changes were small at first, they were real and not illusionary. I felt like someone winning the lottery. Finally I could say with conviction that I can and will change my life for the better.

During this time I continued to fine-tune my affirmations to make them easier to use and more emotionally appealing. Also, I started to prune down the number of affirmations little by little, and sometimes incorporating two into one. As a result, I could focus more and more on each one. I had started off with as many as twelve or fourteen affirmations that dealt with all aspects of my life. Gradually, I whittled them down to just six. I kept only those affirmations that contained some quality that I desired or valued supremely. Of course, it is quite possible to concentrate solely on just one affirmation and devote all my time and energy to it. It would mean achieving a result faster and more completely.

There were various reasons why I did not do this. Firstly, I was probably greedy and wanted to manifest a lot of different changes in my life simultaneously. Also, I could not quite decide which one was my biggest priority. Instead of choosing just one, I wanted to choose all. I also found from experience the advantage of working on a small number of affirmations at once.

Different affirmations take different lengths of time to manifest themselves. Therefore, if you are juggling a few at the same time, some are producing early results while you continue to work on the slower ones. In other words, there is always something happening or manifesting with at least one of the affirmations, which is very encouraging. From then on, there was always something wonderful happening in my life and it continues to this day.

My new pathway through life is constantly under construction with upgrades and I look forward to each new day with a sense of expectation and confidence. There is never a time when you will say, *I will stop now as I have achieved what I wanted.* As you reach one milestone you will always want to move on to the next one. In the earlier stages of my affirmations I discovered the paramount importance of the motivation and enthusiasm necessary to compel my efforts at improving my life. By rereading books on the power of the subconscious mind, I reacquainted myself with its amazing attributes when unleashed by one's own efforts. A powerful suggestion or affirmation that constantly bombards the subconscious always brings results. Remember that the subconscious acts on blind faith. It accepts a strong suggestion without question. Whether that suggestion is true or not makes no difference. That is why when a person constantly thinks, *I have a terrible memory,* the subconscious duly acts to make that a reality. It does not say, *Rubbish, your memory is excellent.*

The Power of Affirmations

An affirmation is a strong positive statement that something has already been achieved or is already so. It is an insistence of what you are imagining. Whether we are aware of it or not, we have an inner dialogue occurring in our minds almost constantly. The mind is conducting a running commentary about everyday happenings, our lives, our feelings, beliefs and attitudes. These ideas and feelings are very important, even though we are mostly unaware of them. They are important because what we are telling ourselves forms our experience of reality. This flurry of thoughts influences and colors our perception of things and ultimately creates and attracts change, for better or worse, in our lives. As an experiment, see if you can stop this constant inner dialogue. Not very easy is it?

There are some very simple laws of affirmations that are necessary to achieve success:

It has to be *positive*. *I am healthy* is correct. *I am free from all disease* is not correct because, even though it means the same thing, it focuses the mind on something that you want to avoid. If you say to yourself constantly, *I must not believe I have a bad memory*, then you are focusing on a bad memory. It must be in the *present tense*. *I will be much calmer in the future*, must be replaced with, *I am much calmer*. What you are trying to convey to your subconscious is that you are already in that situation; it has already happened.

It has to be *realistic* and *achievable* in the short term. When you first begin affirming do not say something patently unrealistic, unlikely or over-ambitious. If you start with modest goals you will realize they are believable and achievable, and then you can move on by aiming a little higher the next time. An exaggerated goal will quickly lead to disillusionment and cause you to cease your affirmations.

Various Methods

There are different ways that affirmations can give you a more positive outlook and help you reach your goals.

1) You can say them silently throughout the day. This method is best when there are other people around, making it impractical to speak the affirmations out loud.

2) Spoken affirmations are the most common and they enable you to use greater emphasis on key words.

3) You can record your affirmations and play them to yourself as you lie in bed, are around the house or while driving the car.

4) You can write down a particular affirmation many times and focus on it as you write. Some people find this most effective.

5) If you have a friend, partner or colleague who wishes to be involved then affirmations can be used as a form of dialogue. You can sit facing each other and take turns in affirming to the other and accepting them.

Example:

Michael: *"Catherine, you are a wholesome, worthwhile, creative and loving person."*

Catherine: *"Yes, I am."*

6) Some people find that singing or chanting affirmations are very effective. They compose their own songs by incorporating their chosen affirmations.

One simple but highly effective affirmation applicable to many situations is; *I definitely can do this.* By repeating this positive statement you will influence your subconscious mind and begin to alter negative beliefs that hindered you in the past. Positive affirmations should become part of your daily routine and eventually become habitual and instinctive. You must remember that most people unconsciously reinforce negative affirmations on a daily basis. To reverse this situation, powerful positive affirmations should become automatic instead. Some people repeat a particular affirmation hundreds of times a day. Experiment at first and find out what most comfortably suits you. You should ideally seek a routine that you can realistically adhere to each day; otherwise there is no continuity, making it difficult to maintain your momentum.

Once you have decided on a particular affirmation or affirmations, look for evidence that supports your statements. This may be difficult at first, possibly because you are not used to looking for what is working for you, but rather what is not working. This, again, is due to habitual negative attitudes. Persevere, however, because results are worth the effort although it may take time. By doing this you are gradually, imperceptibly and profoundly altering your way of thinking. The results are definitely worth the effort. Also, try to refrain from complaining or moaning about trivial disappointments, however annoying they may be. If you find yourself actively grumbling, it is best to stop and restart with your new resolution. This will definitely be difficult at first, but in time you will develop the virtue of positively thinking and speaking. This habit will be the platform for your transformation and the ultimate achievement of your goals.

Summary

1) For maximum effect, affirmations should be repeated in an emotional or animated way.

2) When affirming, persevere, persevere, and persevere

again. It cannot be emphasized too much.

3) By exercising patience and perseverance, one becomes convinced of the system's validity.

4) One should constantly fine-tune chosen affirmations so that they become more powerful and appealing to the subconscious.

5) It is best to work on a number of affirmations rather than just one. Different affirmations may take different lengths of time to manifest.

6) It is very important to remain motivated and enthusiastic, especially in the early stages of affirmations. Reference to books on the power of the subconscious mind should help in this regard.

7) Remember that the subconscious mind accepts strong suggestions without question, whether the suggestion is factually correct or not.

8) Suggestions must be positive, in the presence tense, realistic, and achievable.

9) Affirmations can be silent, spoken, recorded, written, or used as a form of dialogue.

10) Positive affirmations should be used so regularly that they become second nature.

11) When you have decided on your chosen affirmations,

always be on the lookout for evidence that supports them.

Inspirational Words

"The mind is its own place and in itself can make a heaven of hell or a hell of a heaven."
--John Milton

"Think truly and thy thoughts shall the world's famine feed."
--Horatio Bonar

"A man who is master of himself can end sorrow as easily as he can invent a pleasure."
--Oscar Wilde

"You can create your own universe as you go along."
--Winston Churchill

"Change your thoughts and you change your destiny."
--Dr. Joseph Murphy

"Whether you think you can or think you can't, either way you're right."
--Henry Ford

Chapter 4
Affirm for Life

Affirmations should be your constant companions in life. They should become as integral to your existence as breathing. Although unaware before, thousands of thoughts, emotions, and feelings flood through your mind each day. These reflect your attitudes toward all kinds of situations. Some are positive and happy while others are negative and upsetting. If certain feelings, whether positive or negative, become predominant in your mind, they will have a marked effect on your behavior. They act exactly in the same way as affirmations without you being consciously aware of them. Therefore, you are continually programming your mind every waking moment of the day, for better or worse. Unfortunately, most of these kinds of affirmations are negative and are pulling you down, causing you to underachieve. We must stop this random way of stimulating our deeper mind and influence it in a positive way from now on. You must realize that you are the captain of your ship and master of your destiny. You owe it to yourself to fill your mind with positive thoughts and affirmations henceforth. If you do that, your mind will have no room for harmful or destructive thoughts; the two cannot coexist. It is as simple as that.

Constant positive affirmations will become second nature to you. You may think this is difficult or impossible, but it is not. Once you resolve to improve your life and start practicing regularly, you get into the flow of improvement and won't look back. The excellence of affirmations is that they can be easily done at anytime. They can be said as you get up in the morning, have a shower, dress, eat breakfast, exercise and travel to work or school. It will all depend on your circumstances. When you are among company or engaged in something, you cannot do your affirmations very effectively. Therefore, find the times and places which best suit you and integrate them into your daily routine. At the start, consciously use your new affirmations with intensity and enthusiasm until they become permanent in your everyday thinking. They will then easily come to your mind any time you want to affirm. Slowly but surely the new affirmations will replace your old ways of thinking and lead to new horizons.

Sometimes we forget to do our affirmations. The solution is creating little reminders for ourselves. Writing out affirmations on cards or memos is probably the most effective. These can then be put on a mirror, desk or dressing table. They can also be placed in the car to remind you to repeat them as you drive. After constant practice you will not need these reminders as much and eventually can dispense with them if you wish. Affirmations tend to spring to mind regularly even when your mind is not actively engaged. In times of pressure or stress they are reminding you to use them to successfully resolve the situation. This is an indication that your practice has paid off and the favorite phrases are ingrained in your mind. Stressful situations become less fearful now because you know you have a powerful ally to help you. Life takes on a new outlook as you progress with your chosen affirmations and the boundaries of your aspirations are being pushed back all the time. You realize that you are indeed in charge of your life and can bring about the desired changes in an easy and enjoyable way. To reflect your new state of mind the following affirmations may be helpful:

A wonderful life is opening up for me.

Joy and happiness is coming my way.

Universal love is filling my heart.

Every day in every way I am getting better and better.

I am making full use of all my potential.

My life is blossoming more and more each day.

I am master of my destiny.

I am a wholesome and worthy person.

I really like and appreciate myself just as I am.

I transmit love and receive love all of the time.

Summary

1) Affirm constantly throughout the day. Affirming should be as natural as breathing.

2) If you are not actively and consciously affirming positively, you may allow harmful, negative thoughts to run through your mind.

3) Affirmations can be easily done at any time of the day or night.

4) It is beneficial to have reminders of our affirmations written on cards or memos, strategically placed in the house, car or office.

5) Affirmations that are well memorized and used are a powerful ally at stressful times.

6) Life takes on a new outlook when affirmations are done regularly.

Inspirational Words

"Happiness is found in doing, not merely in possessing."
--Napoleon Hill

"Whatever we think about and thank about, we bring about."
--Dr. John Demartini

"Your thoughts and feelings create your life."
--Lisa Nichols

"If you see it in your mind, you will get to hold it in your hand."
--Bob Proctor

"What ever you chose to concentrate on grows in your awareness of it."
--Brian and Sangeeta Mayne

Chapter 5
Self-Esteem

High self-esteem is about having a positive sense of your inherent worth as a person. It is a vital part to a successful, worthwhile and enjoyable life. It involves having a feeling of peace and harmony deep within yourself, while simultaneously respecting others. You mature rapidly as a person when you possess this quality. Your self-esteem is reflected in everything you do. The higher your self-esteem, the better you act. Most people, if they were completely honest, would say that their self- esteem leaves a lot to be desired. Deep down we want more confidence and to feel happier with ourselves. If we are not comfortable with ourselves, generally we try to compensate by putting on a brave face and acting like the coolest people in the world. This is a façade, and it puts pressure on ourselves to be somebody we know we are not and it often leads to stress.

Basically, our behavior and feelings in response to external happenings depends on the way we feel about ourselves. Our negative feelings are the result of the convictions formed in our mind throughout the years regarding the meaning and worth of our personalities. We base our self- esteem on this feeling about ourselves. There is a big difference between high self-esteem and cockiness or overconfidence. High self-esteem does not mean superiority. It simply refers to a happiness and comfort with themselves that encourages the use of potential to the fullest extent. People with high self-esteem are in control of their destiny and do not rely on others to fulfill their ambitions. These people are rare and are to be admired.

I believe that a huge gulf separates people with low self-esteem and people with high self-esteem. The latter are confident in themselves and attract positive things into their lives without realizing it. They breeze through difficult situations, unaware of any problems. Invariably, they are successful in their careers and personal life. They tend to have magnetic personalities drawing other people to them; they have the knack of attracting people to willingly comply with their every wish.

Conversely, people with low self-esteem seem to struggle with most aspects of life, everything appearing to be an uphill battle. They do not make the most of their opportunities, but assume their own failure. Instead of embracing change or challenges they shrink away from them, not willing or confident to benefit from them. Deep down they feel inadequate and inferior, selling themselves short in most situations. Publicly they put on a bold and confident front but privately regard themselves as failures unworthy of success or accomplishment. It is difficult and stressful to go through life trying to disguise your inner feelings and thoughts. You are constantly trying to be somebody you are not. You feel like a fraud and are mortally afraid of the real you being exposed.

I know what this feeling is like and I can certainly empathize with people in that situation because, for much of my life, I suffered with this feeling of inadequacy. In a way, it inhibited and blighted my progress in life. Likewise, it stunted my ambitions and hopes, holding me back in many areas of my life. Fear of rejection and failure was constantly uppermost in my mind. Looking back, I realize that I was only half living while letting many glorious opportunities pass me by.

This conflict or disharmony between the conscious and subconscious mind is the simple reason why so many people are unhappy in life, achieving a small portion of their potential. On the other hand, people with good self-esteem lack such conflict and overcome obstacles of which they are scarcely aware. The good news for the many people with low self-esteem is their ability to easily change their deeply held opinion of themselves. When they get their conscious and subconscious mind to accept that they are worthy and wholesome beings with great potential, then they begin to travel the road to happiness and success.

The most powerful of all suggestions is our self-perception. Therefore, maintaining false perceptions of ourselves is a very strong affirmation. Sometimes a thoughtless comment by a third party only reinforces this belief, affecting all our behaviors. Self-denial effects all our actions and behaviors to reflect this false perception, leading to unhappiness and even misery. The only permanent way of completely changing this deeply held belief is by powerful positive suggestions that penetrate the subconscious. However, before we create our own suggestions, we should ascertain the main feelings we have about ourselves. Then, compose suggestions that will feed off the energy of this feeling. We must try to notice our mentally harsh or critical attitudes towards ourselves and consciously begin being kinder and more appreciative. Try the following affirmations:

I am a decent and wholesome being.

I have talents and intelligence.

I am entitled to the best that life has to offer.

I believe in my self-worth and myself.

I have complete confidence in my own abilities.

I am a unique and worthwhile person.

I like myself and respect others.

Summary

1) Having a good level of self-esteem is a vital ingredient in living a successful and worthwhile life.

2) Lack of confidence in ourselves can lead to pressure and stress.

3) High self-esteem should not be confused with cockiness or overconfidence.

4) People with low self-esteem struggle with most aspects of life.

5) Low self-esteem can stunt hopes and ambitions.

6) The conflict or disharmony between the conscious and subconscious mind is the simple reason that many people are unhappy in life.

7) Luckily, low self-esteem can easily be remedied by affirmations.

8) What we actually think about ourselves is a powerful affirmation in itself.

9) Often a thoughtless comment by a third party can act as a negative affirmation.

10) We must try not to harshly self criticize.

Inspirational Words

"Every failure and adversity brings with it the seed of an equivalent or greater benefit."
--Napoleon Hill

"Just put forth a clear enough request and everything your heart truly desires must come to you."
--Shakti Gawain

"Both poverty and riches are the offspring of thought."
--Napoleon Hill

"Start by doing what's necessary; then do what's possible;

and suddenly you are doing the impossible."
--St. Francis of Assisi

"Means we use must be as pure as the ends we seek."
--Martin Luther King, Jr.

Chapter 6
Stress and Its Relief

Stress is accepted as the most common cause of disease and discomfort in the world. It is blamed for the prevalence of heart disease, high blood pressure, cancer and migraines. The very word disease (or literally dis-ease) means lack of ease or the absence of relaxation. Stress reduces the resistance to disease and contributes to all sorts of social disorders in every strata of society, leading to palpitations, paranoia, strokes, indigestion, hypertension, impotence, constipation and insomnia just to mention a few. It can even lead to suicide. Stress is the cause of more serious disease and suffering than any other condition, and yet the word stress does not sound as sinister as cancer or AIDS. Unfortunately, unlike many ailments, stress does not lessen with time; it is self-perpetuating. It feeds off itself, growing and magnifying the more one concentrates on it. Stress can even escalate a small problem into an insurmountable obstacle in a short space of time.

This reflex or instinctive reaction to problems in our lives is inbuilt into our very nature, and actually exists to help us. Like primitive man we are equipped with a fight or flight mechanism to deal with any emergency or dangerous situation. While deciding whether to do one thing or the other, our bodies are preparing for either eventuality. With no conscious effort, the adrenal glands begin secreting adrenaline and Epinephrine Hormones; these are hormones that respond to stress. Our muscles tense, our heart pounds, our blood pressure rises, digestion ceases and our breathing quicken. In our everyday life every little mishap or problem seems to trigger this fight or flight mechanism and if the situation is not properly addressed we are constantly on edge and are almost permanently under stress. Most people encounter stressful situations dozens of times during the course of a day. Each little aggravation in itself is not very significant, but when all the incidents are compounded the body is in a constant state of alert.

Also, the difference between primitive man and modern man is that the former could resolve a stressful situation by either fighting or fleeing. Thus, stress chemicals produced in his body were dispensed, which allowed him to immediately begin calming down as his stress dissolved and disappeared. However, in modern times, when a person's fight or flight mechanism is activated, he must stay at his desk or at the wheel of his car, forcing himself to appear calm and assured. Straight away there is conflict because he cannot take immediate drastic action like primitive man. Instead, he broods over the situation while his muscles tense and his nerves jangle. As a result, his stress levels rise and the problem continues to compound itself.

Stress in My Life

I had always lived a life full of stress. I was constantly tense and on edge and the more I became aware of it, the more I tried to fight it, and the worse it became. Social occasions were dreaded ordeals to be endured. The tenseness ruined many events that should have been fun. I envied people who were relaxed and laid back because they obviously relished and thrived on these occasions. I always seemed to be on trial and never did justice to myself. When I tried to avoid certain situations by making excuses, I felt disingenuous. I would have given anything to just be myself and enjoy the situation. Does this sound familiar to you?

Outside of social occasions this tenseness continued to affect me. If I worried about something, however trivial, it also caused me stress. In fact, life was full of stress: it was everywhere. Pressures from family, relationships and employment, the ambitions and standards I set myself, my health, doubts, fears and insecurities, were all heavy burdens. I believed that sooner or later I would surely develop very high blood pressure or suffer a heart attack. At times I took a few drinks just to loosen up and relax on social occasions. This was fine, but it was merely a prop and no real solution to the problem. Certainly, it is a real problem with people working under a lot of stress to constantly fulfill high expectations, trying to reach targets and goals almost beyond them. Very often people in the latter category turn to abusing illegal drugs as a way out of their difficulties. However, this leads to all kinds of short and long-term problems.

Most people are unprepared to make major changes in their lives to achieve a stress-free existence. For instance, they are not prepared to change their spouse, their occupation or their geographic location. Similarly, they are not prepared to drastically change their diet, exercise routine or alcohol intake. They believe there is an easier solution to the problem, and of course, there is. When I became convinced of the benefits of affirmations in overcoming stress I could not wait to put my theory into practice. By being totally committed to the concept of influencing my subconscious to achieve my goal, I was able to change my behavior and go through life in tranquility. The process was both enjoyable and easy. It did not cost anything. How many other forms of education can be utilized absolutely free of charge with so great a reward?

Bring as much feeling and emotion as you can to your affirmations. By doing this constantly you are creating experiences that your subconscious will accept as real life situations and will lead to profound change in your life. Strive to have as many relaxed sessions as possible, but regardless keep up the affirmations regularly during the day. Eventually, you will get into a routine that fits into your regular practice of work or other commitments. Find what suits you best. I speak from experience when I say that, when you make a firm promise to yourself to regularly affirm calmness and do so with feeling, you will begin to get results that surprise and delight you.

Do not rush those results or become impatient because, as night follows day, you are changing and becoming a different person. If there appears to be little happening, do not fret-- you are doing nothing wrong. Results and time spans can vary from person to person. You know which affirmations suit your particular needs best. I would just like to suggest a few I found beneficial. For instance, *I am completely calm and deeply relaxed at all times; I am completely immune to all outside influences;* or *I am in complete control of all situations* were all great phrases for me. As you say the affirmations experience the feeling of being relaxed and letting go, similar to the feeling one gets after a few glasses of wine---laid back and without a care in the world. Regular practice with feeling will produce results and encourage you to continue to do so, possibly making you more ambitious in your affirmations.

I noticed that when I found myself in a stressful situation I was waiting for the familiar tightening of the muscles and tenseness, but, to my amazement, it never happened. It was slightly disconcerting. Why am I not tense? Then the penny dropped and I knew I had arrived. Instead of stressful situations controlling my behavior, my behavior was controlling stressful situations. Try this method and you will eventually feel empowered and in control. Life is for living!

I am completely calm and deeply relaxed at all times.

I am totally immune to all outside influences.

I feel relaxed and confident in all situations.

I am very laid back and cool in stressful situations.

Relaxed Stance

While experimenting with calm-inducing affirmations, I stumbled across a method I find very helpful and relaxing, and therefore, worth mentioning. Stand upright with the legs slightly apart and consciously let the body loosen. From the waist upwards bend over forwards and let your upper body totally relax like a rag doll. Bend the knees slightly and let the arms dangle loosely. Allow your facial muscles to relax and let your jaw drop as if you are asleep. Then, gently let both arms sway from side to side while imagining the stress draining completely from your body. As you do this, repeat your affirmations in a low voice. You could say repeatedly; *I am deeply relaxed at all times. Let go, let go, let go.* I have found this procedure extremely beneficial and relaxing and I often begin to yawn while doing it, which is definitely a good sign. I think it is especially helpful if you are anticipating a stressful situation and need a quick fix. Try it!

Summary

1) Stress is a common cause of disease.

2) Stress does not lessen with time; it is self-perpetuating.

3) Stress is inbuilt into our make-up to help us in a fight or flight situation.

4) Modern man often cannot take drastic action in stressful situations and so problems compound themselves.

5) Tenseness and stress can ruin one's social life.

6) Many people under stress turn to prescription or illegal drugs in a bid to overcome their problems.

7) The proper use of positive affirmations is the easy and permanent way to beat stress.

8) You owe it to yourself to influence your subconscious for a better life.

9) Bring as much feeling and emotion to your affirmations as possible.

10) When affirming, do not try to rush results. They will come in their own time.

Inspirational Words

"Life is a gift of nature; but beautiful living is the gift of wisdom."
--Greek Adage

"If we did the things we were capable of, we would astound ourselves."
--Thomas Alva Edison

"Be glad of life because it gives you the chance to love and to work and to play and to look up at the stars."
--Henry Van Dyke

"Our limitations and success will be based, most often, on our own expectations for ourselves. What the minds dwells upon, the body acts upon."
--Denis Waitley

"Embrace uncertainty. Hard problems rarely have easy solutions."
--Jonah Lehrer

Chapter 7
Success

Success is always very high on everybody's wish list. We all want to succeed in one way or another. However, success is a very hard concept to define precisely. There are as many different definitions of success as there are people who try to define it. To me, success means doing something very well that enables me to attain a fulfilling life of contentment, health and abundance. Other people will disagree with that particular concept, but it only proves that success is very individualized. Abundance is one aspect, but it needs to be supplemented. All external forms of success will have little meaning or satisfaction in the long term if inner happiness or peace of mind is absent.

Very often the perception of success lies in luck or monetary wealth. Maybe someone is born into wealth, gets the best education, meets the right people or gets crucial breaks at opportune times. These factors can and do help on the road to success. Successful people manipulate these factors to their advantage. However, it is also true that multitudes of people with little life advantage went on to succeed beyond most people's wildest dreams. Then there are many people who started with obvious advantages but, through a lack of certain qualities, failed abysmally and lost everything. A wise man once wrote that success has three steps. The first step, he believed, is to find out what you most love to do, and then do it. Success, he felt, is in loving what you choose to do. The second step is to specialize in a particular branch of your work and know more about it than anyone else. The third step is to be sure that what you want to do is not selfishly motivated; it must be for the greater benefit of others.

I am now convinced that success has a simple formula. Success is not accidental; it is caused. Lasting success, which is priceless, is achieved through a combination of factors. Firstly, we must know in detail what we want or what we aspire to. This must remain crystal clear in our minds; there must be no ambiguity. Then, and only then, can we focus on our goal with feeling and emotion. We must desire this goal above everything else, unrelenting until we attain it. When we have gained clarity and determination we begin the mechanics for achieving our goal. We must regularly affirm and think successful thoughts; these will trigger actions resulting in genuine success.

Effective visualization is also a vital ingredient used to augment the affirmations. These are indisputable laws of nature and, if religiously followed, will produce the desired results. There is no possibility of failure here; success is assured. It is as definite as the law of gravity.

I am an outstanding success in everything I do.

I easily accomplish every task I have to do.

I am very efficient and dedicated.

People are always happy with the way I do my job.

I am becoming a more successful person in every way every day.

Success is my right and my priority.

<u>Summary</u>

1)   Each of us has a different definition of success.

2)   Being lucky or rich does not guarantee success.

3)   Success has a very simple formula. It is achieved through a combination of factors.

4)   The first step is to know what we want in detail.

5)   We must focus very hard on a clear goal.

6)   Relaxation, visualization, and emotional affirmations are a powerful combination.

7)   When used with conviction these ingredients will ensure success. There is absolutely no room for failure.

8)   The law of success is as definite as the law of gravity.

9)   People who are not successful fail to grasp one or all of these simple steps.

Inspirational Words

"The fragrance always remains on the hand that gives the rose."
--Mahatma Gandhi

"Gratitude is noticing the extraordinary in the ordinary. And then taking the nanosecond to feel it."
--Karen Krakower Kaplan

"Life has been your art. You have set yourself to music. Your days are your sonnets."
--Oscar Wilde

"The more tranquil a man becomes, the greater is his success, his influence, his power for good. Calmness of mind is one of the beautiful jewels of wisdom."
--James Allen

"The only real voyage consists not in seeking new landscapes, but in having new eyes."
--Marcel Proust

"A single act of kindness throws out roots in all directions. They spring up and make new trees. The greatest work that kindness does to others is that it makes them kind to themselves."--Lawrence G. Lovasik

Chapter 8
Money and Riches

Many classics have been written about the science of becoming rich. It is a subject that has always exercised people's minds and will continue to do so. People dream of winning the jackpot in the lottery and, of course, criminal minds are forever full of ideas of getting their greedy hands on a fortune. There is nothing wrong with wanting to be rich. The desire for riches is really a need to lead a fuller, more abundant life. A person without such an ambition leads to an aimless existence. The abuse or misuse of money and riches is the problem. When used properly, money can enable one to lead a fulfilled life with plenty freedom of choice. Having read many books on the science of getting rich, I can summarize some of their conclusions.

Basically, there is a science to becoming rich; it is a very exact and precise science like geometry or algebra. There are natural laws that govern the process of acquiring wealth. Once these laws are understood and put into practice, riches will follow with mathematical certainty. Gaining wealth is not the result of one's environment, saving, thrift or even hard work, but is merely the result of doing things in a certain way.

This begs the question: Is doing things in a certain way difficult? The emphatic answer is "No." People with very ordinary intelligence, as well as highly talented people have become extremely rich. You may not have influential friends, unlimited resources, an advantageous location, or an ideal business. Yet, even with all these apparent disadvantages, if you use the tried and tested formula of influencing your subconscious, success will follow

Authors of classic books on becoming rich have devoted thousands of pages to this subject, and have lectured on the psychology and mechanics thereof. However, in a nutshell, their conclusions have all boiled down to the same few simple laws of nature. They constantly speak of the power of self-suggestion or affirmations in influencing the subconscious to attract what we want and desire in life. They agree that whatever a person regularly repeats to himself, whether true or false, will eventually become believed and accepted as fact. A man is what he is because of the dominating thoughts that occupy his mind.

These writers recommend that, instead of holding negative thoughts, a person must instill powerful positive thoughts, colored with emotion, into his deeper mind. This way he will attract exactly what he wants in life.

Notes of Caution

Some authors give the impression that attaining wealth is quick and easy. In some books, for example, they recommend that you repeat the word "wealth" with feeling just before going to sleep each night. They assert that if you do this, wealth will flow to you in avalanches of abundance. This type of claim is very misleading and will lead to frustration and disappointment. There is a lot more to the accumulation of riches than just being lulled to sleep by one word. Frankly, it amazes me that some authors writing logical and detailed books on the workings of the subconscious mind do not emphasize the importance of patience and perseverance when affirming.

Authors have also accentuated the importance of naming specific amounts of riches we want and the time frame we want them in. I agree that you should tell your subconscious, for instance, if you need just enough money to pay your bills or if you want an extravagant lifestyle with loads of spending power. Regarding time, I believe you should not tie yourself down to a specific, definite time limit. If something is not manifested at the exact time or date you have set, then doubts manifest and again lead to frustration and disappointment.

Gratitude

Some authors constantly stress the importance of gratitude as integral to acquiring wealth. Basically, their explanation is as follows. There is a source from which all things come to us for our benefit. Different people call this source by different names: God, a Higher Intelligence or The Universe. Secondly, this source is capable of giving and wants to give people what they desire in their lives. Thirdly, some people relate to the source with feelings of profound gratitude, becoming more grateful when good events occur. The more they receive and the more rapidly it comes, the more grateful people become.

While doing research, I thought this was a bit of pie-in-the-sky. However, when I put it to the test, I found it really does help, and creates a climate in which good things happen.

Even the Bible encourages us to ask and give thanks when we require something; "Do not be anxious about anything, but in everything, by prayer and petition, with thanksgiving, present your requests to God" (Philippians 4:6-7). This act of faith and belief is as relevant to wealth as in any other area of human life.

Guilt about Riches

Many people want to become rich, but deep down feel guilty about it. Attraction to money makes them feel greedy and uncomfortable. Some believe that by accruing wealth they are somehow depriving others less fortunate. This stems from the belief that riches in the world are limited and if one person has something then another must go without it. This is one of the most common causes of failure. Some who try to affirm abundance and wealth on the one hand, feel guilty on the other. Basically, they are saying; *it is immoral and selfish for me to want riches while others have none.* This is counterproductive because they are affirming scarcity and poverty, compounding the existing problem.

The scarcity concept is false. It is based on a misunderstanding of how the universe works and limits them from realizing their natural state of abundance and prosperity. Of course, many people in the world really are starving and deprived, but we do not need to keep perpetuating that reality. Actually, there is more than enough to go around for everyone if methods for resource distribution change. This earth is a place of great abundance and we were all meant to be prosperous, both materially and spiritually. Unfortunately, this natural prosperity presently does not exist.

Instead, a small proportion of people possess far more

than necessary while the rest live in different degrees of need. We are all partly and collectively responsible for this situation and can only change it by altering our ways of thinking and living. Undeniably, this planet is a fruitful, abundant, and a beautiful place. It is a joy to live in if treated with the respect it deserves. With all our help, it can be transformed into a prosperous and supportive environment where we can all flourish and progress. Unless you commit to this view, you will have difficulty in manifesting the positive benefits you want in your personal life.

To create abundance, imagine yourself living as you desire to live. Be satisfied with your achievements and do what you love simultaneously as others are doing the same. To recap, people need re-education about the concept of scarcity and abundance before they can take the first step on the road to becoming rich. In addition, if people firmly believe it is good and wholesome to have abundance then they can move forward with purpose. Nothing can possibly keep them in poverty. Some affirmations:

This earth is a place of abundance and good things.

I now accept all the prosperity and happiness of the world.

Financial prosperity is flowing to me each day.

I am now prosperous and happy.

The world is a very abundant place for me.

I now enjoy financial prosperity.

I am rich in mind, body, and spirit.

I give and receive freely.

<u>Summary</u>

1) There is nothing wrong in wanting to be rich when it leads to a fuller and more abundant life.

2) It is the abuse and misuse of money that is wrong.

3) Many writers say there is a science to becoming rich.

4) Gaining wealth is not just luck, saving, or even hard work.

5) There are examples of both very ordinary people, as well as talented people, who have gone on to become very wealthy.

6) Basically, acquiring riches is about doing things in a certain way.

7) The findings of authors of classic books can be reduced to a few simple laws of nature.

8) These authors constantly speak of self-suggestion and affirmations to influence the subconscious.

9) These authors also agree that a man becomes what his dominating thoughts are.

10) Authors often give the misleading idea that attracting wealth is achieved quickly and easily. They fail to mention belief, perseverance, will power, and sometimes sacrifice.

11) Gratitude creates a climate where beneficial things happen.

12) Many people mistakenly believe that if they have wealth, other people must go without.

13) Truthfully, there is fruitful abundance for everyone if the planet's resources are equally shared.

<u>Inspirational Words</u>

"It's no coincidence that four of the six letters in health are 'heal'."
--Ed Northstrum

"Never does the human soul appear so strong as when it forgoes revenge, and dares forgive an injury."
--E.H. Chapin

"You are never too old to set another goal or to dream a new dream."
--C.S. Lewis

"Love is always open arms. If you close your arms about love you will find that you are left holding only yourself."
-- Leo F. Buscaglia

"The best way to predict the future is to create it."
--Alan Kay

"A moment's insight is sometimes worth a life's experience."
--Oliver Wendell Holmes

"The best way to pay for a lovely moment is to enjoy it."
--Richard Bach

"Once you choose hope, anything's possible."
--Christopher Reeve

Chapter 9
Health Is Wealth

Health is an essential ingredient of a fulfilled life. All the money in the world is useless without mental or physical health. Everyone needs health to make the most of their existence on this earth. People have always needed healing and at times unofficial healers have obtained remarkable results where authorized medical skill has failed. Some believe this is a consequence of the innate healing power of the subconscious. As observed earlier in this book, if the subconscious accepts something as absolutely true then it will act to create it. A surgeon or physician removes physical blocks to enable healing to flow freely. Likewise, psychologists or psychiatrists remove mental obstructions in a patient so the healing process can begin, thus restoring the patient to health.

Healing and the Subconscious

Amazingly, not only psychologists have the power to transform and change our minds and bodies. Each of us can apply miraculous healing to our mental and physical conditions. This phenomenon is not surprising, as it confirms the principal of the subconscious being influenced to bring about improvements in our lives. Here, it is important to stress that suggestive healing should not replace conventional medical science. Instead, the two should complement each other. It is scientifically proven that the body can often be healed through powerfully focused suggestions. When attempting to heal or improve your condition, constantly affirm that your body is being made whole and being restored to full health and harmony. Equally, if you are in good health you could make the following affirmation; *I am completely healthy and happy at all times.* Avoid mentioning a particular ailment or disease that you may suffer from by name, which may give it undue attention upon which it may thrive.

Why do headaches sometimes go away immediately after taking a painkiller even though it could not possibly have worked so fast? Why does a placebo have such a powerful effect on some people? This very simply illustrates the control the subconscious has over the human body and opens up unlimited possibilities. The subconscious mind is vital to the mental and physical welfare of the body. While you are asleep or awake, the subconscious controls the vital functions of the body. It is responsible for the rhythmic beating of the heart and the continuous inhaling and exhaling of the lungs. Likewise, it controls the digestive process and the functioning of the kidneys and liver, etc.

The importance of the subconscious mind in relation to the functioning of the human body is either unknown or forgotten about until something provokes us to think again. Frequently the conscious mind upsets the smooth working of the subconscious through fear, tension, anxiety, and worry.

This disrupts bodily functions and often causes problems such as upset stomachs, ulcers, headaches, palpitations, etc. When this happens on a continuous basis, the problems are compounded and may lead to more serious illnesses such as high blood pressure and heart disease. Thus, anything interfering with the harmonious functioning of the subconscious should be urgently addressed and remedied.

When people become stressed, tense, overexcited or mentally upset in any way, the only remedy is to take stock, relax, and let go. It is impossible to feel relaxed and stressed at the same time. When we relax the subconscious is allowed to get on with its normal efficient functioning. The word disease means lack of ease and implies that stress can lead to illness. Though unaware of it, our subconscious never ceases working for our benefit unless we, unwittingly, create and perpetuate its mortal enemy, stress.

We should always strive to find time to relax and visualize using different affirmations or combinations of affirmations until we find ourselves comfortable with a few that appeal to us most. Then, we should concentrate on these favorites and use them regularly with feeling and emotion for the greatest effect. Affirmations exercised just before sleeping are the most effective, because the subconscious mind is active during sleep.

Personally, I have affirmed healthy thoughts for a good number of years and am very glad I did so. The funny thing about affirming for health is that when it is working you are not aware of anything different. This is, of course, because you cannot compare your present good health with any other scenario. Other suggestions for health affirmations:

I am presently being healed in mind and body.

Creative intelligence is constantly bringing me health and happiness.

I am being transformed and made whole every minute of the day.

I am alive and whole with boundless energy.

Summary

1) Everyone needs reasonable health to make the most of their existence on earth.

2) Absolute belief often plays a big part in healing.

3) Healing by suggestion should never replace conventional medicine. The two should exist side by side and complement each other.

4) It has been scientifically proven that powerful suggestions can heal.

5) Healthy affirmations can be very beneficial.

6) It is a known fact that the subconscious mind controls the vital functions of the body.

7) Stress seriously impedes the subconscious in its control over our physiology, thus leading to disease.

8) We should make time for relaxation and visualization regarding our bodily wellbeing.

9) Affirmations employed before sleep are most effective.

10) Healthy affirmations are recommended, even when in good health.

Inspirational Words

"There is enough for all. The earth is a generous mother; she will provide in plentiful abundance food for all her children if they will but cultivate her soil in justice and in peace."
--Nietzsche

"To free us from the expectations of others, to give us back to ourselves --there lies the great, singular power of self-respect."
--Joan Didion

"To dare is to lose one's footing momentarily. Not to dare is to lose oneself."
--Soren Kierkegaard

"Learn and grow all you can; serve and befriend all you can; enrich and inspire all you can."
--William Arthur Ward

"The only thing worse than being blind, is having sight but no vision."
--Helen Keller

Chapter 10
Human Relationships

Happy and Unhappy People

Why are some people always happy despite problems in their lives while others permanently see the gloomy side of things and are people you want to avoid? In most cases, if you dig deep enough you will find the unhappy man fills his mind with negative and destructive thoughts. You do not want to be that gloomy, depressing person, do you? Ironically, gloom is instinctive. People do not set out to be thus; that is the way their mind is programmed, over a long number of years, perhaps. However, and for whatever reason, they originally allowed negative thoughts to creep into their subconscious mind in a drip, drip manner. Something could have triggered this attitude--maybe a bad experience or a relationship problem.

I speak from experience when I contend that a person's outlook on life is a result of their predominant thinking, whether positive or negative. For many years my attitude to external happenings was not very positive. For me, the glass was always half empty. I blamed the system, the government, and other people, and generally felt hard done by. I became a martyr in my own mind and always waited for things to go wrong. It was me against the world. As a result of this kind of thinking, I was constantly feeling stressed and resentful. Even when things did not go wrong I was not happy. I was puzzled, feeling that this was not the way things were supposed to be.

From my readings I came to realize that I was acting out a classic case of a person with a negative and destructive attitude toward life. I consciously and deliberately began to try to eradicate this corrosive habit in my everyday life. It was not easy, as the attitude was a long-standing one almost ingrained into my personality. I used affirmations and visualization to radically alter my thinking and attitude. It took time for change to take place but slowly, almost imperceptibly, my reaction to adverse situations became different. I became the master of my own moods. Things still continued to go wrong now and again, and situations did not always turn out the way I wanted, but it did not bother me anymore. I found it easier not to get sucked into stressful situations and just moved on to the next experience. In that way stress no longer controlled me; I was no longer its slave.

I began to feel happier and more optimistic. On the flip side, I know a person who, repeatedly, goes into a rage when certain politicians appear on the television or talk on the radio. He visibly tenses and directs tirades of abuse against these people that irritate him. He fails to see that his outbursts are pointless and counterproductive. The politicians are not affected by his fury but he causes himself continued grief and upset. Unfortunately, he cannot see this and therefore does not rise above it.

Clearly, then, what is important is not what happens to us,

but rather our reaction or response to it. As a result of my affirmations, I was able to take all setbacks and disappointments on the chin and stopped feeling the world was against me. Eventually it became challenging, welcoming every problem that arrived and overcoming it with a smile. However, I finally realized it was my own response or reaction that was faulty in the past, and therefore not anything outside of my control. Thanks to affirmations and visualization, I began breezing through difficult situations without raising my blood pressure levels. I thought it almost comical the way I had behaved at one time. I was allowing situations and people far removed from me, even strangers, to cause me stress and anger. I realized the only person who could hurt me was myself, not anyone else, unless I allowed them to. Some suggestions:

I am totally immune to all outside influences.

I am a happy and content person at all times.

An invisible wall against criticism and hurtful remarks protects me.

Nothing fazes me.

Each day I am getting stronger and happier in every way.

Social Skills

I have found it is possible to improve your social life significantly through affirmations. Also, it is possible to create artificial experiences of social behavior that will beneficially impact your everyday life. We are what we think we are subconsciously. If someone is socially awkward, clumsy, and self-conscious it is because he thinks that he is. It is very difficult to consciously change this way of thinking, and if there is improvement, there is always the risk of slipping back into old patterns. The only permanent way of improving one's social skills is by affirmations and visualization. By doing that, it is possible to convince the subconscious mind that one is socially skilled and good fun to be with. People who feel inadequate in company can eventually and will, positively look forward to social encounters. They are armed with the knowledge that they are socially skilled, charming, and will thoroughly enjoy themselves in any situation. They become sought after in company and will have no shortage of friends.

When affirming that you are good company you must not only use appropriate wording, but also see and feel yourself enjoying the experience. You must imagine people laughing at your jokes and generally responding with great interest and appreciation to what you have to say. Basically you play out an enjoyable social situation in your mind and make it as realistic and believable as possible. I found using audible uninhibited and enthusiastic affirmations coupled with visualizations got the best results. Of course, this should be done in private surroundings--otherwise, it will have to be toned down so as not to alarm or puzzle others.

By performing this method constantly you will get your subconscious to accept the behavior as real. In turn it will enable you to become the person you project. If you feel socially inept and use visualization and affirmations to improve your lot, you will gratefully experience the gradual changes in your behavior. At first you may think that you are just imagining things and everything will revert to normal again. Then it happens again and again, and finally you realize the change is permanent and irreversible. It is a wonderfully magical feeling and you begin craving more affirmations and visualizations to achieve more success.

I have been down this road and am not exaggerating the turnabout; there was a wonderful improvement in my social life as a result of persevering with affirmations and visualization. It is an exciting and continuous journey.

I would like to interject a word of caution here. When you do your affirmations and are achieving results, be happy with them as they come. Do not try to force or speed progress up too much. Trying to do too much too soon could breed disappointment, which will affect your confidence. Act well within you and enjoy each new experience as it comes. Some affirmations:

I am very happy and confident among company.

People find me very witty and amusing.

I am a good conversationalist and listener.

People find me stimulating and attractive.

I am the life and soul of the party.

I bring out the best in other people.

Summary

1) A person's outlook in life, whether happy or gloomy, is the result of their predominant thinking.

2) If a negative outlook prevails, change can occur with the help of affirmations and visualization.

3) What happens to us is not important but, rather, our response.

4) It is possible to improve one's social life significantly through affirmations.

5) Creating successful artificial experiences can produce great benefits.

6) You can convince the subconscious mind that you are socially skilled.

7) When the subconscious accepts repeated, successful, artificial experiences as real then your mission is accomplished.

8) When change is effected, it is permanent; there is no going back.

9) Find happiness with the results; do not try to overreach yourself.

Inspirational Words

"Creativity requires the courage to let go of certainties."
--Erich Fromm

"You have powers you never dreamed of. You can do things you never thought you could do. There are no limitations in what you can do except the limitations of your own mind."
--Darwin P. Kingsley

"Time is a companion that goes with us on a journey. It reminds us to cherish each moment, because it will never come again. What we leave behind is not as important as how we have lived."
--Jean Luc Picard

"A journey of a thousand miles begins with a single step."
--Lao Tzu

"I have been through some terrible things in my life, some of which actually happened."
--Mark Twain

"Eliminate physical clutter. More importantly, eliminate spiritual clutter."
--D.H. Mondfleur

Chapter 11
Anti-social Habits

It is comparatively easy to develop anti-social or bad habits. Most habits, good or bad, start almost subconsciously. They develop and grow with regular usage to become second nature. A lot of bad habits can easily be broken and new good habits formed with a little willpower. However, some destructive habits, such as over indulgence in alcohol, smoking, drug taking, etc. are more ingrained and more difficult to eradicate. People can become heavily dependent on destructive behavior, and for many there appears no way out. They sink deeper and deeper into dependency as the problem continues to compound. Even those consciously trying to overcome the problem by resolving to change their habits have an uphill struggle. They use their willpower to try and suppress their urges, and sometimes succeed temporarily.

A very small number of people succeed in shaking off the shackles of dependency. The majority, after some initial success, loses heart and reverts to their old ways. Repeated failures convince them that their struggle is hopeless and impossible to change. Continually reinforcing this conviction acts as a powerful suggestion, influencing the subconscious in a negative and destructive way. Before I suggest the benefits of using your subconscious mind to free yourself from dependency, I must emphasize that these methods should never be substituted for conventional medical practice. Ideally, the two should go hand in hand.

The solution to overcoming addictive habits can be a surprisingly simple one. Notice I said simple, not easy. The beliefs of the conscious and subconscious mind must be harmonized. A person who has some addiction is in conflict. Consciously, that person desperately wants to stop, but subconsciously, he is convinced he is not capable of doing so. Also, there may be a conflict in the conscious mind where the person, on the one hand, wants to give up, but on the other, really enjoys the pleasure too much and so is doomed for failure.

Therefore, find out what you really and truly desire, be sure about it, and then finally crystallize it into words. Next, compose sentences or phrases that accurately reflect this aspired condition or state. When both conscious and subconscious minds are in harmony the problem is resolved and healing is assured. This may not be as easy as it seems, because sometimes a hidden conflict exists. When you are sure that this is not the case, you can begin to influence the deeper mind with powerful suggestions to bring it in line with your conscious desires.

Alcohol

The main cause of over-indulgence in alcohol is, very basically defined, negative thinking. The alcoholic may have a deep sense of inadequacy, defeat, frustration, or deep-seated anger. He may list many reasons for his excessive drinking, but the real source is his negativity and feelings of inadequacy. An alcoholic is often miserable because he knows his alcohol abuse is causing chaos to his mental and physical well-being, as well as to his family's. There is also a lot of guilt involved. However, if he has a strong desire to free himself from this habit then he is halfway there. If his desire to overcome his problem is greater than his desire for alcohol, he is well on the road to gaining freedom from his predicament. If the mind continues to focus on this freedom and peace of mind, then feelings and emotions are generated which attracts these concepts.

At first it may be difficult, but it is well worthwhile to start visualizing the joy of freedom that lies ahead. This is a form of substitution where once the imagination attracted a person to alcohol it now attracts them to peace of mind, well-being, and freedom. He can heal himself if he is encouraged to devote regular periods of time each day to reprogramming his subconscious. After becoming relaxed he fills his mind with pictures of his ideal state. He sees himself interacting happily in an alcohol-free situation surrounded with the love of his family and enjoying good health. Doing this exercise regularly will recondition his mind and change his perception of himself and his problem. It is a gradual process, but he owes it to himself and his family to persevere. Slowly, the habit pattern of his subconscious mind changes as he achieves success because finally he expects to experience the pictures he creates in his mind. Some affirmations:

I now see myself in a happy and healthy environment.

I no longer feel the need for alcohol.

I see myself in a healthy and drink-free atmosphere.

I enjoy being with my family in full possession of all my faculties.

I enjoy being sober and healthy.

<u>Cigarette Smoking</u>

Due to health issues and warnings, many cigarette smokers wish to cease smoking but cannot. Smoking is a habit people usually develop when they are young. They just drift into it for many reasons, possibly because their friends do it, or it appears a cool thing to do in company. Whatever the reason, it soon becomes an addictive habit. Eventually, however, they decide to quit. It may be too expensive or they become alerted to the health dangers of inhaling cigarette smoke. They then discover that giving up the habit is far more difficult than imagined. For some, it seems impossible. They make many resolutions but repeatedly slip back into their old ways, becoming disillusioned and disheartened. Like the drinker, they develop a failure complex and doubt success. They invest heavily on proprietary brands that promise freedom from smoking. These generally fail because they do not penetrate the root of the problem, which lies subconsciously.

The only sure and lasting way of giving up smoking is, firstly, having a strong resolve to stop. Secondly, is by telling the subconscious you find it easy to give up the craving and are stopping. This way, you are bringing your conscious desire to quit in line with your deeper mind that then accepts that smoking is past tense. The smoker needs to practice relaxing into a comfortable and drowsy state. He then fills his mind with a picture of the desired result while using affirmations to support this projected image. A picture of himself in a healthy and happy cigarette–free environment, coupled with emotion-filled suggestions is the sure way of overcoming his problem. This method does not entail major effort, much willpower, or continued sacrifices, but it does need perseverance and belief. Affirmations:

I find it easy to be cigarette-free.

I am free of addiction and very healthy.

I am healthy and happy being a non-smoker.

I am healthy and saving money without this addiction.

Weight Problems

People who have weight problems are similar to the drinker and smoker. Obesity or being overweight can be a major health problem; it is costly and may be extremely difficult to overcome. As before, sufferers can be driven to despair in trying to resolve their situation. Countless times they may attempt to change their eating habits but each time their willpower was insufficient to persuade them that the health advantages outweighed the pleasure obtained from eating. They know they should moderate their eating but a little voice tells them to carry on, that the instant gratification is irresistible.

As before, they have to be serious about changing their ways, but this should be easy if the habit is costly and unhealthy. They should first regularly practice relaxation techniques to get themselves into a receptive frame of mind. Then they should visualize themselves resisting any desire to overeat. They should see themselves enjoying being a normal weight and all the advantages thereof. Some affirmations:

I am a very healthy and happy person.

I find it easy to maintain my ideal size and weight.

My eating habits always keep me in perfect shape.

I enjoy eating only healthy and wholesome food.

Summary

1) Most anti-social habits are started almost subconsciously and grow with regular usage.

2) Using willpower to shake off an ingrained bad habit is extremely difficult.

3) To overcome addictive habits the conscious and subconscious minds must be in harmony.

4) Negative thinking often contributes to alcoholism.

5) A strong desire to kick the habit is half the battle.

6) Regular periods each day of reprogramming the subconscious mind will bring success.

7) Habitual smokers often want to stop because of health issues and the financial drain.

8) In order to break the habit, smokers must have a strong resolve to stop and also must convince their subconscious of a better alternative.

9) They will succeed when the conscious and subconscious work towards the same end result.

10) The method requires belief and perseverance.

<u>Inspirational Words</u>

"Life is short and we have never too much time for gladdening the hearts of those who are traveling the dark journey with us. Oh be swift to love, make haste to be kind."
--Henri-Frederic Amiel

"Opportunities to find deeper powers within ourselves come when life seems most challenging."
--Joseph Campbell

"If those who owe us nothing gave us nothing, how poor we would be."
--Antonio Porchia

"When we are motivated by goals that have deep meaning, by dreams that need completion, by pure love that needs expressing--then we truly live life."
--Greg Anderson

"Community means strength that joins our strength to do the work that needs to be done. Arms to hold us when we falter. A circle of healing. A circle of friends. Someplace where we can be free."
--Starhawk

'You may be whatever you resolve to be. Determine to be something in the world, and you will be something. "I cannot," never accomplished anything; "I will try," has brought wonders.'
--J. Hawes

"The truth is...everything counts. Everything. Everything we do and everything we say. Everything helps or hurts; everything adds to or takes away from someone else."
--Countee Cullen

Chapter 12
Fear and Its Eradication

We all live with fear in our lives. It is often said that fear is man's greatest enemy. Fear can be behind failure, poor health, and behavioral problems. Large numbers of people are afraid of the past, the future, old age, dying, losing their memory, their mind, etc. Some fears are irrational and have no basis in reality because they are imagined and the subconscious mind inspires a feeling of dread or anxiety in a person's mind. It inhibits them, causing them unnecessary grief and upset. There are many of these types of fear. There is a fear of heights, stage fright, fear of enclosed spaces, fear of flying, exam fear, etc. These fears appear to others as trivial and inconsequential, even downright amusing. They are dismissed as insignificant and unworthy of discussion. However, to the person with such fears and anxieties, they are a very real blight in their life. Fear can paralyze and incapacitate, causing dysfunctional lifestyles.

I understand this type of fear from first hand experience. When I was young, I often froze with fear at meeting people, often feeling inferior to them. It was a terrible and unforgettable experience. There are basically two ways of mastering fear. The first is to face the very thing you are afraid of; by repeatedly doing so, it loses its mystique and sting. Ralph Waldo Emerson, philosopher and poet, said, "Do the thing you are afraid to do, and the death of fear is certain." This method is not easy and requires a lot of courage and perseverance, but it does produce results. With an insight into a particular fear and knowingly influencing the subconscious mind, the problem can be solved in a gentler, easier, and possibly a more complete and lasting way. I freed myself from shyness with this method and thus can speak with some authority on the subject.

Exam Nerves

I knew of a girl who was a brilliant student and was top of her class. However, examinations were a nightmare for her. After assiduously preparing for a test, she often blanked out during examination time. She was confident that she knew the answers but could not recall them back into memory during exams. In the weeks leading up to the exam her mind was full of dread and foreboding and these negative thoughts became charged with fear. Consequently, she was unconsciously requesting her subconscious to ensure failure, and that is exactly what happened, time and time again. She was distraught and repeatedly blamed her memory for letting her down.

With help she learned that her memory was not faulty because it stored a complete record of everything she had learned during her classes. Instead, she was encouraged to change the way her deeper mind was thinking. She was taught how to imprint on her mind a picture of herself celebrating after successful exam results and being congratulated by family and friends. She began to experience the excitement of gaining top marks and the resultant happiness and satisfaction. Basically, she began to anticipate a good end result and the subconscious worked to bring this about. As she visualized her success she reinforced it with carefully chosen phrases confirming for example:

I know I will get the excellent exam results I deserve.

Success is assured for me.

I find the exams an enjoyable experience that will have a successful outcome.

Interviews, Auditions, etc.

Some people who have to speak in public from time to time often go through hell. They dread facing the public and fear humiliation. This fear almost paralyzes them and very often makes a mess of situations. It is similar for interviews, auditions, etc. When an important job or promotion is at stake then the pressure is all the greater. The subconscious mind treats your fear as a request and works to produce this result. If you are fearful of an interview, for example, it becomes an involuntary autosuggestion colored with emotion. This is a very powerful cocktail working to compound your fear and wreck your important occasion.

To create a successful and productive encounter you have to get your subconscious working in accordance with your goal. As you relax, see your big occasion going smoothly, successfully, and enjoyably. See yourself convincingly and in complete control of the situation. Repeat this scenario as often as you can, using appropriate affirmations such as:

This interview (audition) is an enjoyable experience.

I have total confidence that I will be a success.

Success in the interview (audition) is guaranteed.

This interview is a piece of cake.

I will do myself proud.

Fear of Water and Drowning

Some people fear water and drowning. In many cases, this stems from some unpleasant incident in their younger days concerning water. Perhaps they fell into a swimming pool and had the terrifying experience of going under water before being rescued. Maybe they were simply victims of playful pranks involving water. If you are in this category, practice relaxing a few times a day and mentally see yourself happily doing what you presently fear. Make the experiences as real as possible. Feel the cool water and the resistance of it against your arms and legs. Enjoy the experience of gliding through the water with ease and confidence and sniff the fresh air. Make it a memorable experience and use affirmations to confirm this.

I feel safe and protected during my swimming experience.

I love swimming; it is second nature to me.

I look forward to gliding through the water in comfort and safety.

Phobias

Many people suffer from different types of phobias such as claustrophobia (fear of enclosed spaces), agoraphobia (fear of open spaces), and social phobia (fear of embarrassing yourself in front of others). A phobia is a form of anxiety disorder in which someone has an intense and irrational fear of certain objects or situations. Anyone suffering from high levels of anxiety is at risk of developing a phobia.

One of the most common phobias is fear of being in enclosed spaces. A person who has claustrophobia may have an anxiety attack when inside a lift, airplane, crowded room or other confined area. This can cause sweating, accelerated heart rate, and hyperventilation.

The cause of any of these anxiety disorders is thought to be a combination of genetic vulnerability and life experience. With appropriate treatment, it is possible to overcome claustrophobia or any other phobia.

Treating phobias relies on psychological methods. Depending on the person, some of these methods include flooding and counter-conditioning. Flooding is the method where a person is deliberately brought face to face with what they fear most until the anxiety attack passes. By facing the fear, they come to realize that it cannot harm them. This can be a powerful form of therapy. Counter-conditioning involves the use of specific relaxation and visualization techniques when experiencing phobia-related anxiety. In a relaxed state people see themselves acting and reacting in a positive and confident manner when confronted by their phobia. They see themselves treating the situation as insignificant and trivial while moving on with their life. This is known as systematic desensitization. The affirmations should confirm that they have already overcome the problem with confidence, success, and optimism for the future. Some affirmations include:

I feel secure, protected and loved every day.

I am in full control of my mind, body and spirit.

I release the past; I live in peace and happiness.

I relax into the flow of life and let life flow through me with ease.

From day to day all my personal problems are dissolving and disappearing.

Summary

1) Everybody lives with a certain amount of fear in his or her lives.

2) For some, fear can paralyze and incapacitate.

3) A way of mastering fear is by confronting it directly.

4) The other method is by employing your subconscious mind to see that a particular fear has absolutely no substance.

5) Negative thoughts can ensure an excellent student will not pass her exams.

6) Only by getting the subconscious to anticipate a good result can she do herself justice.

7) If one is fearful of an interview, that fear can act as autosuggestion for failure.

8) An irrational fear of water can be overcome by relaxation and pleasant visualization exercises.

9) A way of treating phobias is by deliberately bringing people face to face with that which they fear most.

10) The gentler method is to use creative visualization to dispel the fear.

Inspirational Words

"Think of giving not as a duty but as a privilege."
--John D. Rockefeller Jr.

"You never change something by fighting the existing reality. To change something, build a new model that makes the existing model obsolete."
--Buckminster Fuller

"There is a universe in the sound of every voice, and if you're a patient listener, you can often sense the heartbeat in the long silences between the words."
--Neenah Ellis

"Only in quiet waters do things mirror themselves undistorted. Only in a quiet mind is adequate perception of the world."
--Hans Margolius

"All the statistics in the world can't measure the warmth of a smile."
--Chris Hart

"A person's world is only as big as their heart."
--Tanya A. Moore

"The great blessings of mankind are within us and within our reach; but we shut our eyes, and, like people in the dark, we fall foul upon the very thing we search for, without finding it."
--Seneca

Chapter 13
Guilt and Forgiveness

Most people make mistakes and have regrets. These mistakes are easily rectified and people learn and benefit from them. Unfortunately, some misguided actions have far-reaching knock-on effects and repercussions. Some could lead to a feeling of anger and the desire for revenge to even things out and solve the problem. However, revenge very often creates suffering and hardship, not only for the victim but also for the perpetrator. Even though the latter feels justified in retaliation and retribution it severely disturbs peace of mind and creates conditions for further suffering and self recrimination. The avenger finds that his retaliatory actions have not, in the long run, given him any satisfaction, but rather added to the suffering already done. This creates all kinds of guilt that can lead to regret, resentment, bitterness, conflict and unhappiness.

Most people, if they were honest with themselves, will admit to harboring a certain amount of anger and/or regret in their lives. They may be nursing an old grievance against somebody or feel guilt for treating someone badly. These emotions hold people back from enjoying a fuller and happier existence. The only way to move on and be healed is forgiveness. If one feels hurt by something done against them, they must learn to forgive that person. If one feels guilty or ashamed of something they did, they must forgive themselves.

All around us we see examples of people who go through life in an unhappy state because of feelings of guilt and resentment that blight their lives. They behaved badly at some stage in their lives, usually when they were young, and unconsciously have been punishing themselves ever since. They believe they do not deserve to be happy and fulfilled because of what they have done. They also become cold and hard in their dealings with others and generally have a chip on their shoulders. They are desperately unhappy without really knowing why.

Others bear grudges, real or imagined, and these feelings hold back and inhibit them in most aspects of their lives, preventing them from any real happiness or fulfillment.

They must be taught how to forgive, either themselves or others--that is the only way forward. They must be shown that bitterness and negative hurtful memories block the free flow of life and impede healing. They must also learn that forgiveness is difficult, and often it is easier to forgive others than oneself. It will take a lot of thought, reflection and generosity. However, the prize is huge: it is the gift of peace of mind and contentment.

Experts agree that relaxation and visualization are vital ingredients in the rehabilitation of people hurt by guilt and anger. The first steps to healing are to use visualization and relax properly. People must improve their self-esteem and reduce anxiety. Doing this induces healing as well as giving insight into their thoughts and feelings. Relaxation and visualization are of paramount importance in healing emotions and preparing for forgiveness. In a relaxed state you reflect on all your negative feelings and how they affect your life.

Let all kinds of thoughts surface--do not repress, let them all pour out. Take as long or often as you require: it is the first step in the healing process. Secondly, reflect on what your life might be like if you were to change your attitudes toward your present predicament. What would the word forgiveness mean to you? Do you think that you could bring it into your life? What are your feelings towards the person you wish to forgive? Do you think that you could actually forgive them? Continue to ask yourself any questions that drift into your mind. Focus clearly on the kind of life you live today and how happy or unhappy you are with it. Next, visualize the kind of life you could have if you absolutely forgave this person and moved on with your life. How would your life change if you were not dwelling on that person's wrongdoing, and instead spent your time on more rewarding activities?

Visualize a scenario where you are free of these negative and harmful thoughts and are blissfully doing something that brings you great happiness. See this new life as clearly and as detailed as possible. Feel the freedom and carefree abandonment as you pursue new challenges and achieve new goals. Enjoy this mental scene, letting it envelop you as you bask in its warmth. When you finish your relaxation and visualization process you will understand and picture a life of forgiveness and acceptance. Remember this image, and retrieve it any time you want.

This experience should prove very effective in the healing

process. It should be repeated regularly to set you firmly on the road to freedom. Gradually adjust your visualization to include the person who offended you. Realize that your continued anger will do neither of you any good, but forgiveness will help both of you enormously. As you begin to forgive see it expanding you, making you strong and wholesome. See yourself letting go of anger and resentment, replacing it with patience and tolerance. As the negative feelings subside realize that these were causing upset, disturbance and unhappiness in your life.

Remember that forgiveness is not about dismissing the perpetrator from their wrongdoing; it is about freeing the victim. Once you forgive you can more easily forget the infraction and no longer concern yourself with it. Consequently, a great burden will be lifted so you can concentrate on the future.

Suggestions for Forgiveness

I fully and freely forgive.

I release him/her mentally and spiritually.

I completely forgive everyone connected with this incident.

I am free and he/she is free.

I release everybody who has ever hurt me in any way, wishing them happiness and peace in their lives.

I release you and wish you every blessing in your life.

<u>Summary</u>

1) Everybody makes mistakes in their lives; however, some people's misguided actions have far-reaching effects and repercussions.

2) Very often the perpetrator, as well as the victim, suffers as a consequence of wrongdoing.

3) Feelings of guilt can lead to regret, resentment, bitterness, conflict and unhappiness.

4) Often, the only way to move on and be healed is through forgiveness.

5) Forgiveness is given to others or to oneself.

6) Real or imagined grudges can inhibit people, making happiness or fulfillment almost impossible.

7) Relaxation and visualization are of paramount importance in emotional healing and preparing for forgiveness.

8) Relaxation allows negative suppressed feelings to surface and be released.

9) Visualization is used to see what kind of life is possible if forgiveness is introduced.

10) This pleasant experience should prove very effective in the healing process.

11) Forgiveness is not just about pardoning the perpetrator from wrongdoing; it is also about liberating the victim.

<u>Inspirational Words</u>

"We should be too big to take offense and too noble to give it."
--Abraham Lincoln

"When all is said and done, the only change that will make a difference is the transformation of the human heart."
--Peter Senge

"The value of achievement lies in the achieving."
--Albert Einstein

"What we have done for ourselves alone dies with us; what we have done for others and the world remains and is immortal."
--Albert Pike

"The food that enters the mind must be watched as closely as the food that enters the body."
--Patrick Buchanan

"Each of us has much more hidden inside us than we have had a chance to explore. Unless we create an environment that enables us to discover the limits of our potential, we will never know what we have inside of us.
--Muhammad Yunus

Chapter 14
Sleep and Inspiration

Sleep is almost as important as breathing to us. We spend approximately eight hours a day or one third of our life asleep. It is a natural state of bodily rest. However, not everything rests during sleep. Our heart, lungs and vital organs continue to function, as well as, our digestive system and constantly active subconscious mind. Sleep is vital for our normal successful functioning and when we awake we feel refreshed. Our conscious minds get involved in worry, strife and stress each day and it is very necessary to withdraw from such vexations. Lack of sleep causes us to become moody, irritable and depressed. Sometimes severe insomnia has even preceded psychotic breakdown. However, the purposes of sleep are only partly clear and are still the subject of intense research.

The most effective affirmations are those done immediately before sleep. During sleep the creative mind works on these affirmations without interruption from the conscious mind, producing powerful results. Also, if you have a problem bothering you and seek a wise solution, you need not go any further than your subconscious. On many occasions I have encountered some seemingly impossible situations with no apparent way out. Before sleep I have slowly gone over the problem in my mind and consciously asked my subconscious mind for an answer. I always had absolute faith that my subconscious mind would find a solution and generally, by the next day, the problem would be solved.

When you worry, you are holding mental pictures of things you do not want, instead of things you do want. So, as you go to sleep, visualize the ideal condition you are seeking, instead of the one existing. Then realize that when asleep, your subconscious mind has the opportunity to work on the problem. After surrendering my problem over to my subconscious I settle down to sleep, confident that everything would be sorted out for the best. This method has always worked for me and the solution to my problem would come in a flash of insight a day or two later. Try it! If you do not have a problem but just want your business to thrive you can also give instructions to your subconscious for the attainment of that goal. You simply say, for example; *while I am asleep, my subconscious mind will decide the proper steps I should take in increasing the sales of my product and expanding my business. I will be guided accordingly.* This apparent magic happens because the intuitive faculty of the subconscious mind is able to deliver the solution.

Inspiration

Inspiration is an elusive concept. We are aware of its existence but find it hard to define. Sigmund Freud and other psychologists located inspiration in the inner psyche. Other psychologists and philosophers, such as John Locke, believed ideas associate with each other and that a string in the mind can be struck by a resonant idea. Therefore it appears inspiration is a somewhat random but wholly natural association of ideas and sudden unison of thought. Everybody agreed that this burst of insight comes directly from the subconscious mind.

Inspiration causes men to compose great symphonies that touch everybody who listens to them. Poets can draw on deep inner resources to compose beautiful lines of poetry. An artist can produce a masterpiece on a blank canvas or a songwriter can put melody and lyrics together to form a memorable and lasting song. But, where does this inspiration come from? Where do great inventors get their ideas from and from whence do playwrights get their plots? It comes from their subconscious minds and often comes in a flash of genius or intuition. We may not be groundbreaking psychologists or philosophers, but we can also use our deeper mind to create inspiration.

Our subconscious mind is a creative goldmine from which we can prosper at any time, if we learn to tap into it. In fact, we often do this without realizing it. For instance, if we have some problem and are desperately looking for a solution we turn it over in our minds many times. As the answer is not forthcoming we forget about it and move on to other events. Suddenly, out of the blue a simple and perfect answer presents itself that resolves the situation. Thankfully, everyone can tap into this hidden and bottomless reservoir of talent by communicating effectively with our constant companion, the subconscious. As we become aware of its workings we can enlist its help in inspiring us, whenever we need to. The best time to ask for help is just before we go to sleep at night.

Do relaxation exercises to get into the right frame of mind and then review the situation in all its complexities. Gently affirm to the subconscious, the seat of creative intelligence, that we cannot solve things alone. Therefore we are turning our problem over to it with complete confidence and trust in the knowledge that a perfect solution will be found. Creative people concerned with patentable ideas, designs, story material, subjects for paintings, etc., will frequently find their mind to be most active at bedtime, when ideas appear thick and fast. Countless and well-known people have received help from their subconscious mind when faced with a problem or lack of ideas. They hand over the query and get on with their other work, happy in the knowledge that a perfect solution will result. For example, Robert Louis Stevenson, the novelist, revealed that he regularly sought help from his subconscious mind when he ran out of ideas and needed an exciting storyline for his book. It never let him down, he said, and he could not claim credit for much of his brilliant writing. The credit was due to his subconscious mind.

If we follow this writer's example, we can constantly direct a substantial flow of ideas and suggestions into our consciousness that will benefit our business and social lives as we become innovative and resourceful. Some suggestions:

My mind is a magnet for ideas that will improve my business.

I am always receptive to new ways of doing things.

I let my subconscious mind inspire me at all times in all necessities.

When I am asleep I am being enlightened and guided.

I now ask my inner mind to solve this problem for me; I have complete faith in it.

I am happy in anticipation of my continuous growth and achievement.

Summary

1) Sleep is absolutely necessary as a state of bodily rest.

2) The purposes of sleep are not fully understood and are still the subject of intense research.

3) Affirmations are best and most effective when done immediately before sleep.

4) Sleeping on a problem does actually work.

5) Commands given to the subconscious immediately prior to sleep are very powerful.

6) The answers to problems often come in a flash of insight when least expected.

7) The reason behind apparently magical answers is that the intuitive faculty of the subconscious is able to bypass the objectively known facts of the conscious mind.

8) Inspiration is an elusive concept, but can empower people to brilliance.

9) Thankfully, all of us can tap into this hidden and bottomless reservoir of talent by communicating effectively with our subconscious.

10) Like great writers and poets, we can constantly direct a substantial flow of ideas and suggestions into our consciousness that will benefit our business and social lives.

Inspirational Words

"Don't walk in front of me, I may not follow. Don't walk behind me, I may not lead. Just walk beside me and be my friend."
--Albert Camus

"A single question can be more influential than a thousand statements."
--Bo Bennett

"The final piece of reaching for authentic power is releasing your own to a higher form of wisdom."
--Gary Zukav

"Man is a creature of hope and invention, both of which belie the idea that things cannot be changed."
--Tom Clancy

"Do not consider any act of kindness insignificant, even meeting your brother with a cheerful face."

--Muhammad

"There are two ways of spreading light: to be the candle or the mirror that reflects it."

--Edith Wharton

"Listening is such a simple act. It requires us to be present, and that takes practice, but we don't have to do anything else."

--Margaret J. Wheatley

"Life is a celebration of awakenings, of new beginnings, and wonderful surprises that enlighten the soul."

--Cielo

Chapter 15
The Power and Awe
of the Subconscious Mind

Very few, if any of us, realize or appreciate the wonderful gift we have, the subconscious mind. Much is not known about it and it is often shrouded in misconceptions, but we do know that it has awesome beneficial power if used properly. Unfortunately, it can also be harnessed to create havoc in people's lives. The subconscious is a difficult subject to discuss because of our lack of knowledge about it. Also, because it possesses mysterious quality that tends to intimidate people and causes them to dismiss it as nonsense. Therefore, the subconscious has unwittingly become a divisive force. The best advice to the non-believers is to suspend judgment and give it a sporting chance.

Those who have accepted the existence of the subconscious and experienced its power and effectiveness, never fail to be amazed by the life-changing benefits it brings. Its potential to profoundly change and convert people's desires into reality is almost beyond comprehension. I believe that at all times it should provide a warning reading, "handle with care!" The only limitations to subconscious achievements are the limits imposed by people's own beliefs. To harness your inner mind and make it your genie in the bottle, a few simple steps must be followed.

<u>Desire</u>

The first step in achieving or acquiring some desired characteristic is a simple one; we must know what we want. This should not simply be a matter of saying, "I think I would like this or like to become that." The particular desire should be indelibly imprinted on your mind and you should want it above everything else. People are advised to be absolutely clear about their goals and to write them down. There must be no ambiguity.

It may be hard at first to decide on what quality or qualities you desire. Most likely, you will change your mind a few times. This is a normal part of the process of selecting your goal. The important thing is to ultimately choose something that will persevere, through thick and thin. When you reach this stage you have reached your first important milestone.

Everybody *wishes* for things all the time. However, *wishing* for something will not bring results. It is the *desiring* something almost to obsession and coupled with persistence that is vital. People must be serious enough to burn their bridges to achieve what they truly want. They must not accept defeat at any cost. Only then will they have successfully taken the first step.

Communicating with the Subconscious

Next, we have to communicate our desire and determination to our subconscious mind in order to achieve goals. This is, in effect, transferring thoughts from our conscious to our subconscious mind. As earlier shown, this is done by emotion-charged affirmations and visualizations. Through dominating thoughts that one deliberately holds in the conscious mind, access is gained to the deeper mind, or the subconscious.

We have total control over the kind of thoughts that reach our subconscious through our five senses. Thus, the choice is ours. Do we allow constant negative thoughts to create a negative charge in our deeper mind, or do we deliberately choose powerful positive thoughts that we know will change our future? Remember, our subconscious is like a rich fertile garden in which weeds will grow in abundance if the seeds of nourishing vegetables are not grown there. We must choose to grow our choice of crops with the help of positive affirmations rather than allow the weeds to flourish through neglect and constant unguarded negative thinking.

At this stage it may be helpful to reread Chapter 2 about affirmations and their use. Through the constant use of emotion-charged affirmations you communicate your most ardent desires to your inner mind in a spirit of absolute faith. Initially, it may be advantageous to read aloud your written affirmations until they become crystal clear. When they are committed to memory they can be used at any time. They should be used with emotion and conviction.

Whatever the object of your desire is, you must see and feel it as if it had already happened. If you affirm for money then you must see it and believe that it is already in your possession. This may not be easy at first, but if you affirm constantly with a blind faith you will obtain whatever it is you want. The importance of faith or belief cannot be over estimated. It is faith that gives power, life and action to the impulses of thought. Faith is vital to achieving all our aims and goals and without it we are rudderless. As the old saying goes "Faith will move mountains." Because faith cannot be analyzed by the rules of science we just have to trust it. Countless numbers of people are glad they did!

When conditioned properly the subconscious will accept whatever the conscious mind tells it without question. Though it may appear dishonest or faintly ridiculous to suggest something that is patently not true (yet), it is the way to proceed. Logic has to be suspended for the time being and with constant conditioning the subconscious will accept without question what it is being told and will act in a powerful way to manifest your desires.

It is very important to fully grasp and understand what is contained in the last paragraph. It is precisely because many people do not appreciate the principles of affirmations that they fail to achieve success and do not get the results they had hoped for. They say they have tried it but it does not work. The simple fact is that they did not understand the principles involved and their efforts were doomed from the start.

It is important to realize, and it is worth repeating here, that ordinary, unemotional words or phrases will not influence the subconscious mind. You will get little or no results until you communicate with your deeper mind with feeling, emotion and conviction. It may take time to achieve this but do not let that dishearten you, because it usually takes practice to get things right. The reward at the end is so great that the effort made to successfully influence your subconscious is a small price to pay. You cannot cheat in your dealings with your subconscious and expect to get results. It will not work if you tell your inner mind that you are wealthy but are not convinced of it. Many enthusiastic people have affirmed wealth over and over again but nothing happened. Upon closer examination it was found that, although they kept telling their subconscious that they were rich, deep down they did not really *believe* it. Their conscious and subconscious were in conflict, thus guaranteeing failure.

For some skeptics it may be best if they lowered their aim at first and affirmed for something that did not require as much blind faith. In that way, they would gradually gain trust in the system before they try something more ambitious.

Your ability to be successful with your affirmations may depend on your capacity to turn a desire into a burning obsession. When this happens it is almost impossible not to influence your subconscious in a successful and fruitful way. As you continue to feed your inner mind with powerful emotional affirmations you will *know* that you are doing things correctly. To recap, if you have a burning *desire* for something and actually *believe*, you *will* have it.

It is often said that man is master of his own earthly destiny. However, it does not explain why this is so. The reason why man *can* be master of his earthly destiny is because of his capacity to influence his subconscious mind. Realistically, and unfortunately, only a tiny minority of people exercises that capacity.

It is worth remembering that the subconscious mind functions whether one makes the effort to influence it or not. Thus, involuntary negative thoughts such as fear or poverty will serve as a stimulus to the inner mind. Therefore, individuals owe it to themselves to ensure that deliberate positive thoughts are constantly fed to it instead. The subconscious cannot remain idle and if you do not tend to it properly, then it will digest the thoughts it receives as a result of your neglect.

Strive to cut off the flow of negative thoughts to your subconscious by replacing them with permanent positive impulses. This is of paramount importance. Hopefully, you will eventually succeed and when you do, you can finally choose what your inner mind focuses on; instead of being its slave, you become its master.

Remember that everything you produce or create begins as a thought. You can create nothing that you do not conceive in thought form. Through your imagination, these thoughts are often organized in the form of plans. When these plans are charged with positive emotion and then presented to the subconscious, they are on their way to manifestation.

Repetition

A very necessary ingredient in the whole mix of successful manifestation is repetition. This may not be blindingly obvious at first, but without it nothing will be achieved. Like mantras or prayers, thought impulses have to be repeated over and over again to impact the subconscious mind. Repetition is irresistible. Take a drop of water for instance. One drop will make no impression on a slab of limestone; neither will a hundred or even a thousand. However, over a length of time rainwater will corrode and leave a very noticeable mark on the limestone.

Similarly, when a seed is planted in the soil it requires watering. The watering process goes on for some time with no evidence of anything happening. However, with time and perseverance the moisture will affect the seed, causing it to spring into life and produce a new plant. Thus, repetition can turn something small into something very effective.

There is no substitute for repetition. However, there are two ways of repeating something, one as in prayer and the other as a mantra. In a mantra, words or sounds are repeated over and over again with no thought given to their meaning. In prayer, however, for greatest effectiveness, each word and sentence is said with full awareness of its meaning. Prayers said mechanically without thought are totally ineffective.

We should treat our affirmations as an effective prayer. It is very easy to slip into the habit of repeating our affirmations during the day in perfunctory fashion. This is very understandable and we are all guilty of it from time to time. It is important to realize that words or phrases repeated in a parrot-like way are just a waste of time. It is only when sentiments are expressed with full meaning and emotion that they are efficacious.

Just to repeat a word of caution mentioned earlier in this book; it can get a little tedious doing your affirmations and visualizations over and over again with little apparent results or improvements. That is why it is helpful to keep motivating yourself and assuring yourself that all the effort is well worth it in the long run. There are many well-written books on the capabilities of the subconscious mind to encourage you when your spirits are a little low.

Summary

1) The subconscious mind has an awesome power if used properly.

2) A burning desire is the first step towards achieving a goal.

3) We have total control over the thoughts we allow to reach our subconscious mind through our five senses.

4) Through the constant use of emotion-charged affirmations you communicate your most ardent desires to your inner mind in a spirit of absolute faith.

5) If you affirm constantly with a blind faith you will obtain whatever it is you want.

6) The reason why man is master of his earthly destiny is because of his capacity to influence his subconscious mind.

7) People owe it to themselves to ensure that deliberate positive thoughts are constantly fed to their subconscious mind.

8) Everything you produce or create begins as a thought.

9) A necessary ingredient in the whole mix of successful manifestation is repetition.

10) It is helpful to keep motivating and assuring yourself that all the effort is worthwhile in the long run.

Inspirational Words

"What we plant in the soil of contemplation, we shall reap in the harvest of action."
--Meister Eckhart

"We can't change the cards we're dealt, just how to play the hand."
--Randy Pausch

"Every child is an artist. The problem is how to remain an artist once we grow up."
--Pablo Picasso

"Everything has beauty, but not everyone sees it."
—Confucius

"Keep a green tree in your heart and perhaps a singing bird will come."
--Chinese Proverb

"Most people don't recognize opportunity when it comes, because it's usually dressed in overalls and looks a lot like work."
--Thomas Edison

"To be truly radical is to make hope possible, rather than despair convincing."
--Raymond Williams

"The mind has exactly the same power as the hands: not merely to grasp the world, but to change it."
--Colin Wilson
"To be surprised, to wonder, is to begin to understand."
--Jose Ortega y Gasset

"His high endeavors are an inward light, that makes the path before him always bright."
--William Wordsworth

Chapter 16
Visualization

Visualization is a powerful and effective tool in influencing the subconscious mind. It is simply imagining yourself in some ideal circumstances or attaining something you have always wished for. It is most effective when done in a very relaxed state. It can take a relatively short time or quite a considerable length of time. It should always be an enjoyable experience to indulge in your dreams, wishes and fantasies. To add to the effectiveness of the visualization, selected positive affirmations can be added, either aloud or silently.

It is important to learn to relax properly when you first start to practice visualization. The inner mind is at its most receptive when in a calm and composed state. At such a time images, messages and suggestions have a greater impact on it. The advice given in Chapter 2 regarding the different steps to relaxing should be followed.

Many people take to creative visualization straight away. However, others find it a little more difficult and may need some guidance. In most cases, the people with difficulties are the ones that tend to over analyze the simple method and then worry they are not doing things properly. For instance, some have great difficulty in actually seeing the mental images they desire when they are relaxing. Because of this, they believe they are not getting any real benefit out of the method. They also believe there is a correct way of doing it, and they are not doing it adequately.

They can be readily reassured on this point that they are in fact doing nothing wrong. It is a very individual experience. Some people can, in fact, see very vivid images with their mind's eye while others just sense things or are aware of them. We all use our imagination constantly to "see" things and do not worry about the form they come in. It is the same with visualization, just enjoy the pleasant experience as naturally as you can and with practice you will easily master the method.

Creative visualization is effective because it gently and powerfully influences the subconscious mind to produce favorable results in its own time. When in a relaxed state, the inner mind is at its most receptive; you are its master and it awaits your command. This is the opportunity to impress upon it your most wished for circumstances or what possessions you covet most of all. To say the genie awaits your command is not an exaggeration. The power of the subconscious cannot be over estimated.

Visualization coupled with relaxation gives us the unique opportunity to create our own artificial or synthetic experiences that the inner mind accepts as real. The enormity of that fact is amazing. It allows us to manufacture experiences that will benefit us greatly in whatever field we choose. It is the same as creating virtual experiences in the privacy and comfort of our own homes so that we can face real life difficult situations in the future confidently. Let's take an example; I am scared stiff of public speaking and I would dearly love to do it

118

in a calm, authoritative and relaxed manner. Instead of enduring many nerve-wracking and humiliating attempts in front of live audiences, which may kill off my ambitions, I opt instead for creating my own successful sessions in front of an imaginary group of appreciative people. Before each session I get myself completely relaxed and begin my visualization process. After relaxing thoroughly, I see myself striding confidently onto the stage or platform. I immediately put the tentative audience at ease with a joke or some witty remarks. I then launch into my speech with enthusiasm and humor, keeping my listeners spellbound and very appreciative. When I finally finish my speech the audience is on their feet and I get a long-standing ovation.

Sounds a bit crazy? Maybe, but if it helps me to speak in public with confidence and conviction, who cares? Of course, the above exercise must be repeated time and time again to impress itself on the inner mind and turn images into reality.

In an ideal world we would have loads of time to find an ideal place to relax in and perform our visualization exercises many times a day. However, we are not in an ideal world. Therefore, affirmations can come to the rescue when visualization exercises are not possible. They are very flexible, very powerful, and can be easily used to plug any gaps that arise. Certainly, visualization used in conjunction with affirmations form a very powerful tool in positively influencing the subconscious mind.

Summary

1) Visualization is a powerful and effective tool in influencing the subconscious mind.

2) To add to the effectiveness of the visualization, selected positive affirmations can be made either aloud or silently.

3) It is important to learn to relax properly when you first start practicing.

4) Some people can, in fact, see very vivid images with their mind's eye while others just sense things or are aware of them. Either way is fine.

5) Creative visualization is effective because it gently and powerfully influences the subconscious mind to produce favorable results in its own time.

6) When relaxed, the inner mind is at its most receptive. You are its master and it awaits your command.

7) Visualization and relaxation allows the unique opportunity to create our own artificial experiences.

8) Visualization allows us to manufacture experiences that will benefit us greatly in whatever field we choose.

9) The artificial experiences must be repeated time and time again to impress themselves on the inner mind.

10) Visualization, along with affirmations, combines to form a very powerful tool in positively influencing the subconscious mind.

Inspirational Words

"When a deep injury is done us, we never recover until we forgive."
--Alan Paton

"Be an opener of doors for such as come after thee."
--Ralph Waldo Emerson

"Even hundredfold grief is divisible by love."
--Jareb Teague

"There is more hunger for love and appreciation in this world than for bread."
--Mother Teresa

"Good is the transcendence of self in service to others."
--Michelle Nunn

"It is not because things are difficult that we do not dare, it is because we do not dare that things are difficult."
—-Seneca

"Leaders are more powerful role models when they learn than when they teach."
--Rosabeth Moss Kantor

"In giving you are throwing a bridge across the chasm of your solitude."
--Antoine de Saint-Exupéry

"One's first step in wisdom is to question everything - and one's last is to come to terms with everything."
--Georg C. Lichtenberg

"To think is easy. To act is hard. But the hardest thing in the world is to act in accordance with your thinking."
--Johann Wolfgang Von Goethe

Chapter 17
In Conclusion

We wonder why some people are successful and happy while others always appear unlucky and troublesome. Why are some prosperous and contented while others poor and miserable? Why does one man have the Midas touch while another man works hard for a mere pittance?

At this point, one should have a better understanding of the laws of nature regarding the subconscious mind and be better able to answer the above questions. It is easier to see that, unlike the popular belief that luck is the key, we can be the architects of our own success and masters of our own destiny. Armed with a working knowledge of our inner mind and a determination for improvement, we should have no failures if we believe we are realizing our full potential. Whether the harnessing of the subconscious mind for our benefit is a new concept, or whether we were always aware of its potential but it never appeared to work for us, we owe it to ourselves to master the basic steps and principles outlined in this book. Do you think the end justifies the means?

Some years ago, I tried the system haphazardly on a few occasions, and knew I was at the crossroads. I decided to give it one last genuine effort to make it work. If that effort failed, then I would just forget about the whole process and, instead, concentrate elsewhere. Thankfully, after a ponderous start, things began to fall into place for me. Looking back on it now, I am so glad and relieved that I decided to give affirmations and visualizations one last chance. I am glad because it has completely transformed my life and continues to do so. I am also relieved because I was so close to giving up on something so amazing and beneficial. I have nothing to gain from persuading people to take the affirmation and visualization processes seriously, but I feel obliged to urge them to do so in order to enrich their lives as I have done.

Before plunging in and getting carried away by the hype they read about influencing the subconscious mind, they should instead completely immerse themselves in its natural laws and rules. When they familiarize themselves with those laws, they will be in better position to judge if the system is compatible with their busy lives. Believe me; it will take a lot of time, patience and practice to do justice to the system, as well as, perseverance and some sacrifice.

I believe that great numbers of people enthusiastically throw themselves into practicing affirmations and visualizations, but only a comparatively small number see it through to fruition. I was in the former category on a number of occasions and that is why I believe I can view the situation from both sides of the fence.

My advice, for what it is worth, is to be realistic about improving your life and changing your circumstances. If you want this goal more than anything else and are genuinely prepared for a long, and at times lonely, road ahead, then you can, and you will, succeed. There is no doubt about it. Your success is guaranteed and I and countless others are witness to that.

I am averse to refer to the "miracle-working power" of the subconscious. I believe it casts the subconscious into the realm of the fictitious, and gives the impression that it is all "pie in the sky." Influencing the subconscious mind for success in our lives is achieved by taking advantage of basic laws and rules of nature. There is nothing supernatural or miraculous about it.

As mentioned earlier, it is best to thoroughly understand the system first. Take as much time to do this as is necessary. When this is achieved, experiment with many affirmations until you feel comfortable with the ones that suit you best. Next, use regular sessions of affirmation and visualization to gradually introduce emotion and animation into those sessions. Eventually, when you feel you have mastered the technique, add a very important ingredient to the mix.... commitment. Basically, at this stage, there is no going back. You will persevere until you accomplish your goal. This is where you burn your boats.

The road is going to be a long and rocky one, but are you going to be put off by minor setbacks? If not, you will be rewarded. Resolve to stay on the straight and narrow path at all times. Thankfully, many happenings will reassure and encourage you. These little successes will undoubtedly strengthen your journey as you experience change and growth. You will realize that the changes are permanent and there is no going back.

Affirmations and visualizations should be an ongoing and permanent part of your life. The new roadway through life that you are building should always be under construction. When you accomplish one goal, enthusiastically move on to your next and the one after that. Hopefully, you can attract into your life great health, happiness, wealth and joy after learning to communicate with and release the hidden power of your subconscious mind. Begin to recognize the potential of your deeper mind and cooperate with the laws of nature for a fuller, more fulfilling life.

You should recall once more the analogy of the gardener tending his garden. You are the gardener with the responsibility of sowing seeds (conscious affirmations) in the soil of your garden (subconscious mind). If you are a conscientious gardener you will endeavor to sow the best quality seeds to create a good productive harvest and a rich return for your time and care. On the other hand, if you are careless and inattentive with your gardening, weeds will begin to take hold and grow, eventually strangling the good plants. The garden then will not be a pretty sight. Are you going to be a good gardener or a careless one? My final recommendation to you is to *believe*. Did you ever hear of the saying, "Faith will move mountains?"

He told them, "I tell you with certainty, if you have faith like a grain of mustard seed, you can say to this mountain, 'Move from here to there,' and it will move, and nothing will be impossible for you."(Matthew 17:20)

Inspirational Words

"We make a living by what we get, but we make a life by what we give."
--Winston Churchill

"Education is not the filling of a pail, but the lighting of a fire."
--William Butler Yeats

"Anything that has real and lasting value is always a gift from within."
--Franz Kafka

"There is no success without hardship."
—Sophocles

"If you want to see an endangered species, get up and look in the mirror."
--John Young, former Apollo astronaut

"After silence, that which comes nearest to expressing the inexpressible is music."
--Aldous Huxley

"There is nothing more uncommon than common sense."
--Frank Lloyd Wright

"Time makes more converts than reason."
--Thomas Paine

"Trust everybody, but cut the cards."
--Finley Peter Dunne

"Concentration is the secret of strength."
--Ralph Waldo Emerson

Chapter 18
Questions and Answers

The following are some questions that people who are new to affirming tend to ask. I answer each question as honestly as possible.

Q) Some sources claim that affirming or visualizing bring about fantastic changes in one's life and fortunes. Are these claims not just a little exaggerated?

A) No. When the principle is understood properly and practiced with perseverance and feeling, the results are indeed amazing. Sometimes people promoting the virtues of affirmations make it sound miraculous and far-fetched. This can be a turn-off at times and gives the impression that the whole concept is mere mumbo-jumbo. The experiences of people who have seriously tried the system find out that the results go beyond their expectations.

Q) How much time should be given to affirming and visualizing?

A) The more often it is practiced the better the results. Each person has different circumstances and must put aside a little time regularly when it suits them best. It is recommended that a session of five to ten minutes be completed four to five times a day. It is advisable to design a routine and thus be less liable to miss a session. The good thing about practicing on a regular basis is that, after some time, the results manifest themselves and the practice does not become an ordeal, but rather something to be looked forward to. As the saying goes, *"success breeds success."*

Q) How long before I begin to feel the benefits of practicing affirmations?

A) There are no hard and fast rules for this and results will vary from person to person. Do not expect instant results or you may be disappointed. If you persevere, the results will most certainly come and encourage you to greater efforts. However slow the results are in coming, do not throw in the towel. Every positive thought and affirmation of yours is making an impression on your subconscious mind and is steadily working in your favor. No affirmation ever goes to waste. It is only when they manifest themselves that you see the evidence. Remember, your mind is like an iceberg; only the tip is perceived but a lot is happening beneath the surface. So continue and persevere because you are making progress even if unaware of it.

Q) Are affirmations best said quietly or aloud?

A) This is a matter of personal preference and each person must discover which way suits themselves best. Personally, I find that my surroundings will dictate which method I use. When out walking alone I find that affirming out loud is very effective and can be done with feeling. Obviously, when you are indoors or in company, it is best to be discreet. Some people find it advantageous to affirm aloud in front of a mirror when they are cleaning their teeth. It is a matter of horses for courses.

Q) Can I change my affirmations or do I have to stick to the original ones?

A) You start with affirmations that express your desire best and you are happiest with. If a better affirmation presents itself early on, then it is advisable that you switch. Then you persevere with it until it becomes second nature with continued usage. Later on, the only time you change your affirmations is when you feel you have attained your goal. At that stage you aim for a more ambitious goal and adjust your affirmations accordingly. In fact, it is rare that a person starts with an affirmation and sticks rigidly to it because change usually dictates new wording to reflect that change.

Chapter 19
Soothing Words from Scripture

The following are the words of the Psalm 23, which always had a profound effect on me:

The Lord is my shepherd: I shall not want. He maketh me to lie down in green pastures, he leadeth me beside the still waters.

He restoreth my soul: he leadeth me in the paths of righteousness for his name's sake,

Yea, though I walk through the valley of the shadow of death, I will fear no evil: for thou art with me, thy rod and staff they comfort me.

Thou preparest a table before me in the presence of mine enemies: thou anointed my head with oil; my cup runneth over.

Surely goodness and mercy shall follow me all the days of my life: and I will dwell in the house of the Lord forever.

For many years I have repeated this piece of Scripture every now and again when I feel disappointed or upset at someone or something. Its words never failed to bring me great comfort and consolation. In turn, I thoroughly recommend it to anyone who is going through a rough patch. I am convinced it has a powerful therapeutic and calming effect on the human mind. I believe it is almost impossible to read it slowly and not be uplifted by it.

It is only a short psalm and can be easily memorized. I strongly urge the reader to repeat the passage slowly a number of times each day. If one feels the need, they can increase the frequency to suit their requirements. I have occasionally spoken to people about its efficaciousness. After using it for a short while, they all unanimously praise its deep healing power.

I believe that if recited or read slowly on a number of occasions each day, this psalm will bring great calm and peace into a person's life. It is important to read slowly dwelling on the meaning of each word, allowing it to sink in. Try it!

Psalm 23, supposedly written by David, represents a powerful and positive approach to everyday life. It emphasizes the importance of faith and trust in the Shepherd. The Shepherd knows each one of his sheep and guides and protects his flock. The psalm reassures us that we are not alone but are cared for and cherished. If you find it beneficial, then you may also derive comfort from Psalm 91, also a very powerful piece of writing. As with the last psalm, it is best to read it slowly and thoughtfully, letting each word sink in. The psalmist is confident that God's presence will protect the people who trust in Him in every dangerous situation:

Psalm 91

He that dwelleth in the secret place of the most High shall abide under the shadow of the Almighty. I will say of the Lord, He is my refuge and my fortress: My God; In Him will I trust.

Surely He shall deliver thee from the snare of the fowler, and from the noisome pestilence.

He shall cover thee with His feathers, and under His wings shalt thou trust: His truth shall be thy shield and buckler.

Thou shalt not be afraid for the terror by night; Nor for the arrow that flieth by day;

Nor for the pestilence that walketh in darkness; Nor for the destruction that wasteth at noonday.

A thousand may fall at thy side, and ten thousand at thy right hand; but it shall not come nigh thee.

Only with thine eyes shalt thou behold and see the reward of the wicked.

Because thou hast made the Lord, which is my refuge, even the most High, Thy habitation; there shall no evil befall thee, neither shall any plague come nigh thy dwelling.

For He shall give His angels charge over thee, to keep thee in all thy ways.

They shall bear thee up in their hands, lest thou dash thy foot against a stone.

Thou shalt tread upon the lion and adder; the young lion and the dragon shalt thou trample under feet.

Because He hath set His love upon Me, therefore will I deliver Him: I will set him on high, because he hath know My Name.

He shall call upon me, and I will answer him: I will deliver him, and honor him.

With long life will I satisfy him, and show him my salvation.

Some final words of inspiration to uplift and enlighten us as we continue our journey through life:

> "Dance as though no one is watching you.
> Love as though you have never been hurt.
> Sing as though no one can hear you.
> Live as though Heaven is on Earth."
> —Old Traditional Prayer

Further Reading

Dr. Joseph Murphy, *The Power of Your Subconscious Mind* (London: Simon and Schuster, 1988), 4 .

Peter Fletcher, *The Power of Auto-Suggestion* (Northamptonshire: A. Thomas and Company, 1973), 4.

Shakti Gawain, *Creative Visualization* (California: New World Library, 2002), 1V.

Napoleon Hill, *Think and Grow Rich* (New York: Ballantine Books, 1996), 4.

Rhonda Byrne, *The Secret* (Oregon: Beyond Words, 2006), 1V.

Brian and Sangeeta Mayne, *Life Mapping* (London: Random House, 2002), 1V.

Dr. Wayne W. Dyer, *You'll See It When You Believe It* (London: Arrow Books, 2005), 1V.

Dale Carnegie, *How to Win Friends and Influence People* (Surrey: World's Work Ltd., 1977), 1V.

Acknowledgments

I wish to thank everybody involved in the production of this book. The manuscript editor, Allison L. Skoglind was a pleasure to work with for her efficiency and courtesy. Also, thanks to Stella Jackson of American Book Publishing, whom I found most helpful and co-operative.

Thanks to my own family for their patience and advice while writing the manuscript.

Finally, a word of gratitude to the DailyGood email service for permission to include many of the quotations at the end of the chapters, which I am sure, will be an inspiration to all.

About the Author

Thomas Finn lives in southern Ireland. He is an accredited Life Coach with a special interest in NLP. For many years he has been interested in reading practical psychology publications. He is particularly interested in self-development, self-help, and especially the vital role that the subconscious mind plays in realizing one's full potential.

He is also an artist who works with oils and acrylics. He mainly does landscape and portrait painting. His website is **www.tomfinn.ie.**